Uncle Josh's Outline Map Book

Mark-It Maps for All Subjects

by George Wiggers and Hannah Wiggers

Cover Design:
George Wiggers

Photographer:
Kim Whitmore

Editors:
Cindy Wiggers, Maggie Hogan

General Instructions:
Cindy Wiggers

Published by GeoCreations, Ltd.
Dover, DE 19904

Uncle Josh's Outline Map Book

Mark-It Maps for All Subjects

First Edition
Copyright © 1999 George W. Wiggers and Hannah L. Wiggers
All maps in this book are copyrighted. Copyright © 1999 by Geography Matters, Inc.

Publisher: GeoCreations, Ltd.

Printed in the United States of America
Library of Congress Catalog Card Number: 99-71678
ISBN: 0-9663722-1-2

To order or distribute this book contact:
Geography Matters, Inc.
P.O. Box 92 • Nancy, KY 42544
(800) 426-4650

Uncle Josh's Outline Map Book
Mark-It Maps for All Subjects
Table of Contents

Acknowledgements

Special thanks to Schwindel Graphics, of Evansville, Indiana, for all of their valuable time and computer advice. To David Broad of Digital Wisdom for the fantastic cover art. To Maggie Hogan for editing, inspiration and consultation. To Hannah for helping me in this collosal project. I want to thank my family for allowing me to neglect them for a season. Most of all, thanks to my wife, Cindy, for all of her help and efforts in making this book possible. Ad maiorem Dei gloriam!

---Josh

First of all I would like to thank God for giving me the patience to finish this project. Thanks also to my dad for helping me to do my best and to Mom for believing in me and encouraging me to do this.

---Hannah

4

Uncle Josh's Outline Map Book

General Instructions

You hold in your hand a whole world of learning opportunities for your students! Hannah and I have selected over one hundred outline map titles designed to add fun and adventure to any school subject. Kids love using maps, especially when they get to draw and color in events about which they are currently learning. You'll be amazed at how much more they remember, when a mapping activity is coupled with your history, literature or even science lessons.

Here are some suggestions to get you going.

History

- Draw explorers' routes and include a drawing of the flag representing the country that sponsored each explorer. Color code routes and draw or connect a picture of the type of ship used by each explorer.

- Record boundaries of lands conquered, territories established, new frontiers explored, etc.

- Use maps as an integral part of your lesson plans. Simply introduce each new subject by using the appropriate map(s) and labeling them with pertinent information. Add more data as your study progresses.

Geography

- Draw and label major rivers, lakes and other bodies of water.
- Draw physical features using colors as seen in good classroom atlases.
- Copy appropriate thematic maps from atlases using color coding.
- Label countries, states, capitals and major cities.

Literature

- Select a map representing the area you are studying and label all places of importance.
- Label surrounding countries, states or territories.
- Find and label major sources of water, transportation routes or movement as depicted in the literature selection.
- Compare and contrast the climate and terrain in your story to the student's place of residence.
- Map the action in the story, if appropriate.

Science

- Study the weather and hurricanes with maps.
- Map geological regions and natural resources using color coding, or different markings such as slashes, dots, triangles or shading.
- Use maps for learning about volcanoes, earthquakes and other earth science topics.
- Don't forget maps when learning about the oceans and the water cycle.

Helpful Hints for Amazing Activities

Regardless of what subject you find to use with your maps, these suggestions will help students organize their information and produce fine looking map assignments.

Helpful Hints for Students

- Color code, use pictures, symbols and small stickers when possible.
- Make a legend of all markings.
- Plan to use a variety of atlases, as well as using maps in textbooks, as resources for mapping activities.
- Use a current world atlas to get accurate information for your maps.
- Start with pencil, then mark over pencil with fine-tipped markers. or colored pencils when you are satisfied your work is correct.
- When possible, words should be written horizontally.
- Label grid lines with accurate latitude/longitude degrees.
- North is toward the top of the page unless otherwise indicated.
- Be creative, you have great ideas yourself!

Helpful Hints for Teachers

- To find specific maps in my book, use the table of contents. If you don't see what you're looking for, think about the area. For example, you'll find Croatia on the Balkans map. Do you need Northern Ireland? You'll find it on the map titled British Isles. Keep looking. Believe me, every nook and cranny of the earth is on at least one of the maps in my book!
- Be prepared: have adequate resources on hand before giving a map assignment. I highly recommend providing your students with a current world atlas. See the back of this book for suggestions and ordering information.
- Have students orient the map in the same way it is oriented in the atlas they are using. Adding their own compass rose might help.
- Finding large bodies of water or other stand-out features first makes labeling easier.
- Encourage students to use maps with posters, reports and class demonstrations.
- Feel free to enlarge any section of these maps. (We don't "blow up" countries, we enlarge them.)
- These maps are copyrighted, but I want your students to learn. So make as many copies as you need for your own personal use. Copying is permitted for families, co-op classes, or one classroom - NOT for an entire school.

Uncle Josh's Special Map Features

I've put some special features in these maps to make using them more interesting. You'll notice that most of the maps have rivers lightly shaded. It's not necessary for students to label all of the rivers! Select those of importance to your study, trace in blue and label. Grid lines depicting latitude and longitude are included where possible. This helps students to better identify where these places are located on the surface of the earth and to compare them to places for which they are already familiar. Also, oceans and larger bodies of water are shaded to enhance reference points, making the outlines easier to use. (You may need to darken the setting on your copy machine for the shading to show.)

We've made every effort to make these maps as accurate as possible. Because of map projections, some maps may be distorted. If a boundary is missing, hey, it's an outline map - draw it in! If a boundary changes somewhere in the world, try liquid paper or white out before making copies. If you find an error, feel free to contact me and I'll gladly correct it on the next printing of this book. (My email address is: geomatters@earthlink.net)

Well, there you are. Go for it, and have fun exploring the world through maps!

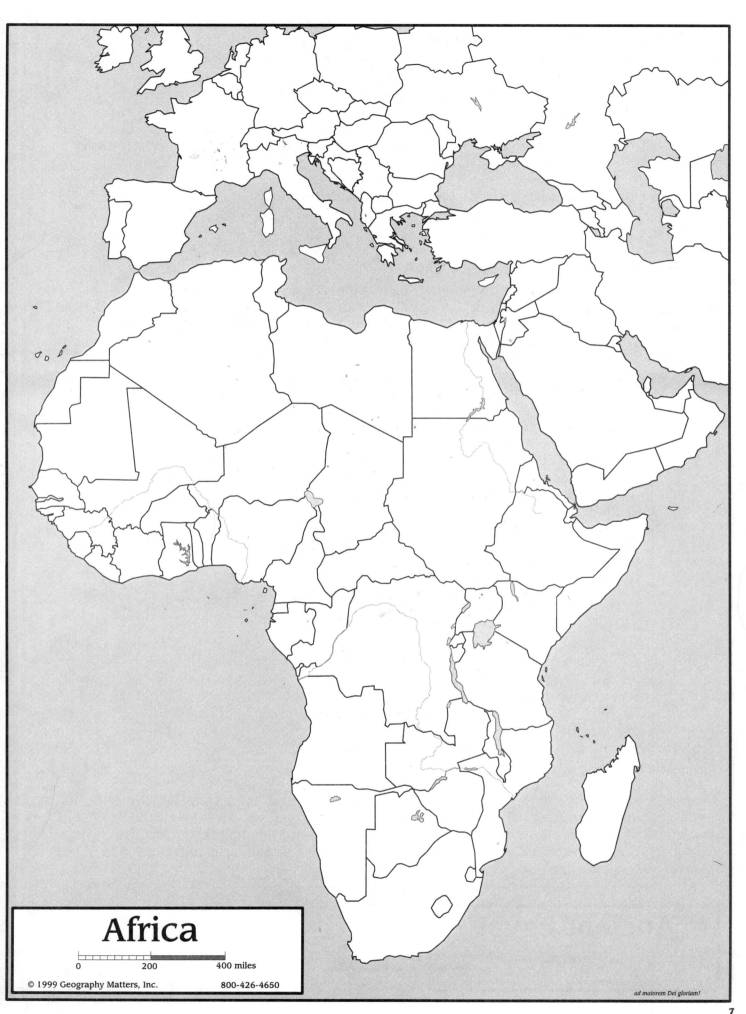

Africa

0   200   400 miles

© 1999 Geography Matters, Inc.   800-426-4650

ad maiorem Dei gloriam!

7

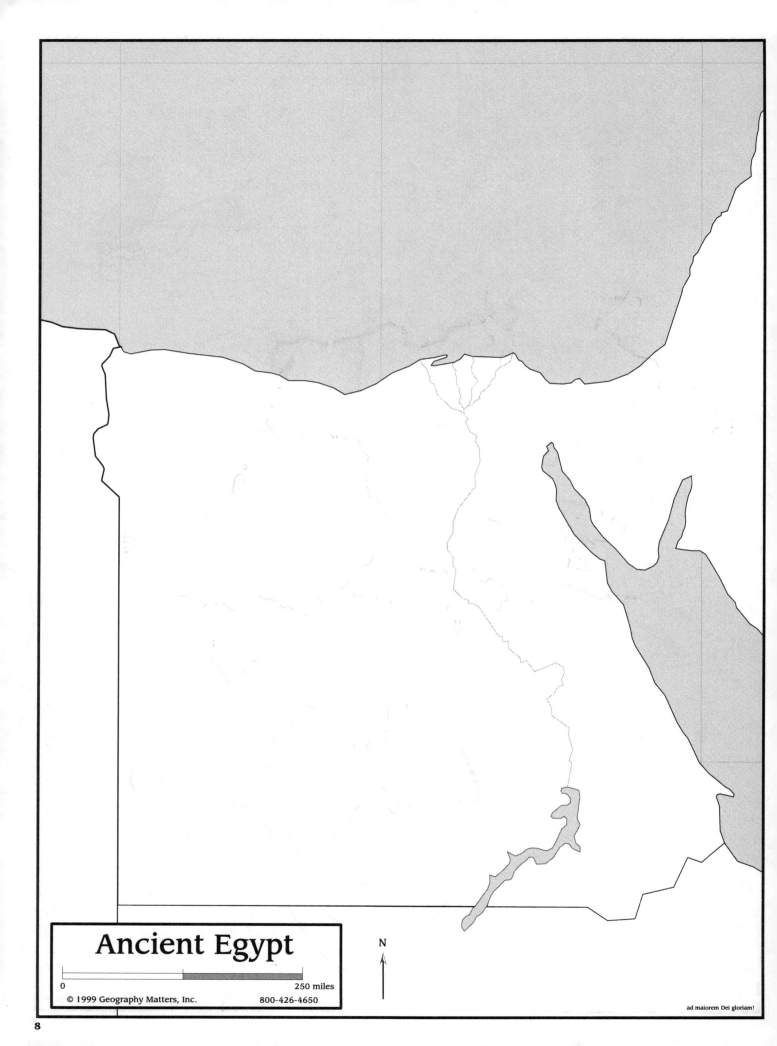

Ancient Egypt

0   250 miles

N

ad maiorem Dei gloriam!

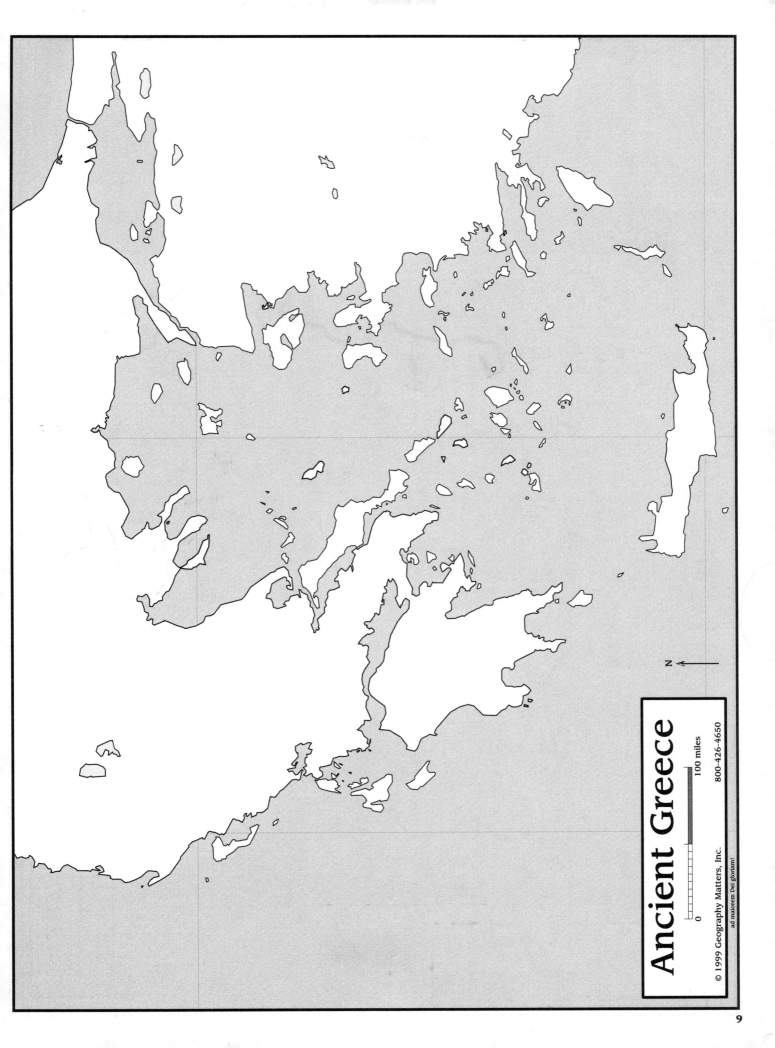

Ancient Greece

N ←

0 [scale] 100 miles

© 1999 Geography Matters, Inc.

800-426-4650

ad maiorem Dei gloriam!

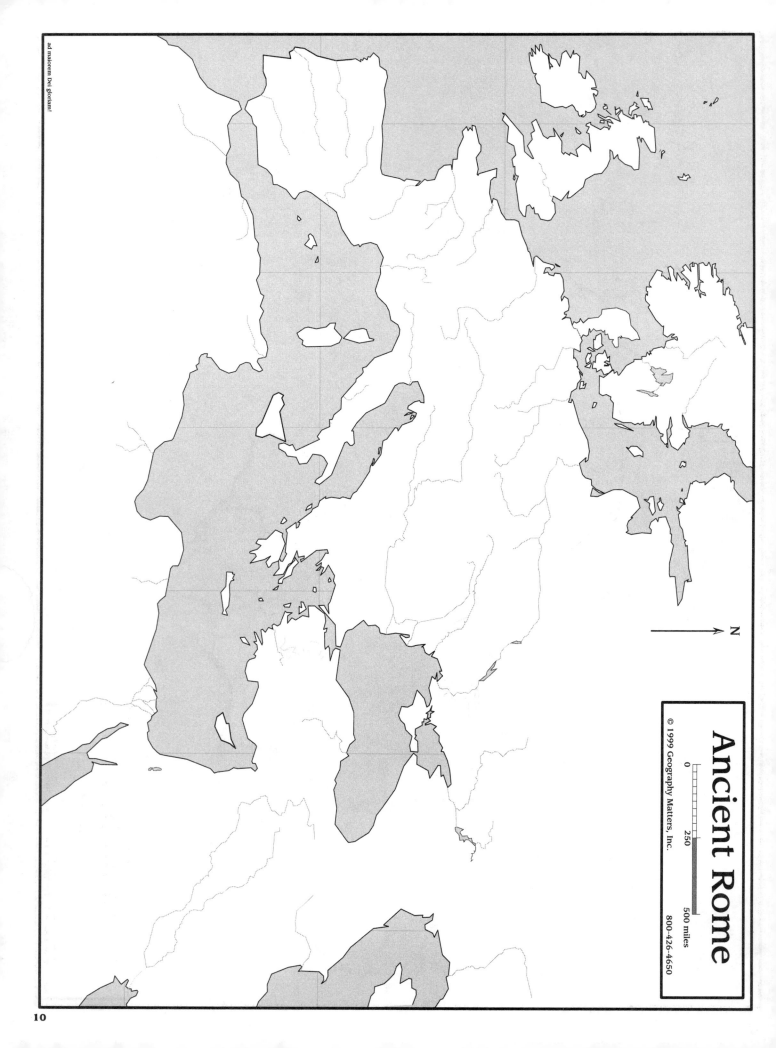

Ancient Rome

© 1999 Geography Matters, Inc.

0   250   500 miles

800-426-4650

N

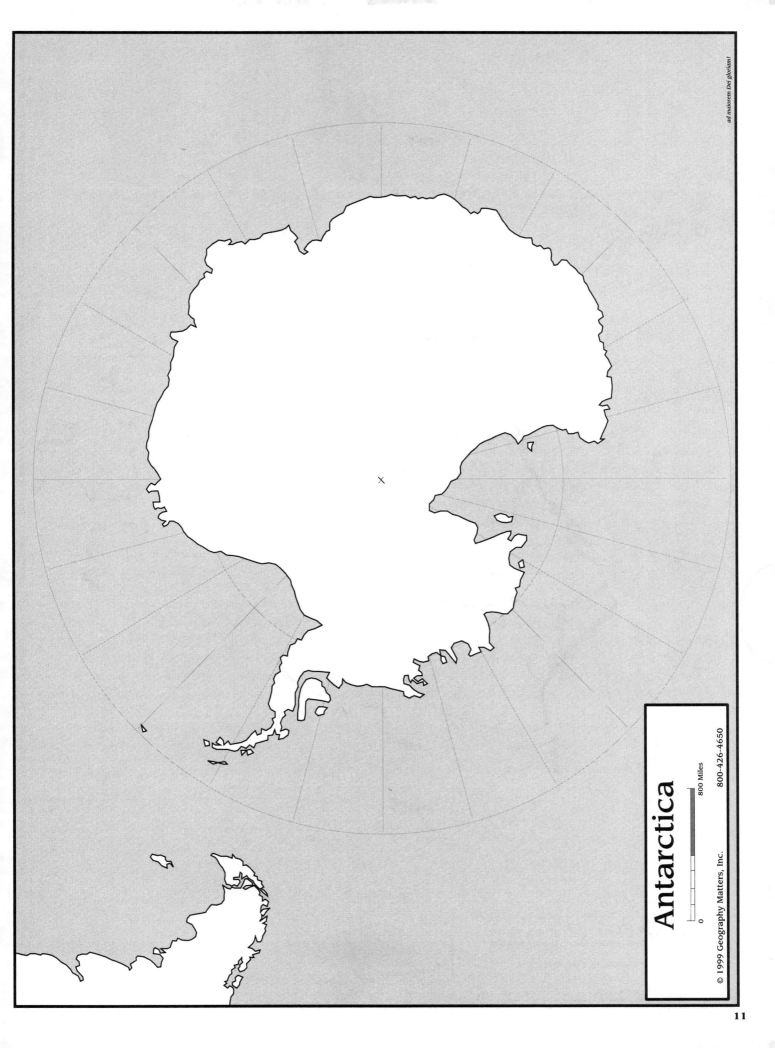

Antarctica

800 Miles

0

© 1999 Geography Matters, Inc.

800-426-4650

ad maiorem Dei gloriam!

11

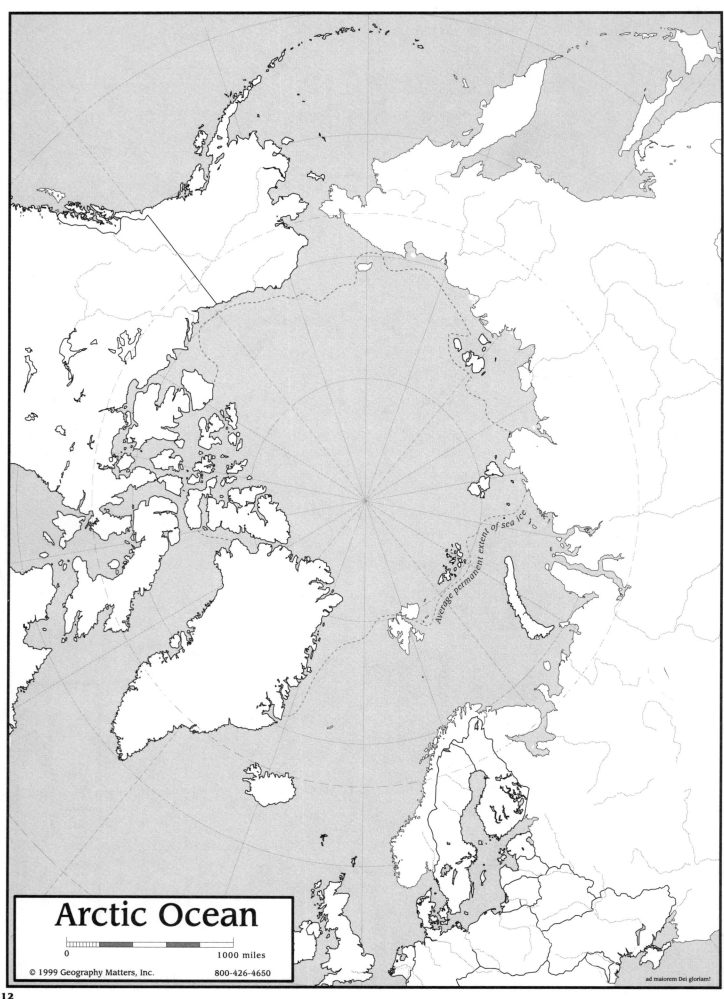

Arctic Ocean

Average permanent extent of sea ice

0   1000 miles

© 1999 Geography Matters, Inc.   800-426-4650

ad maiorem Dei gloriam!

12

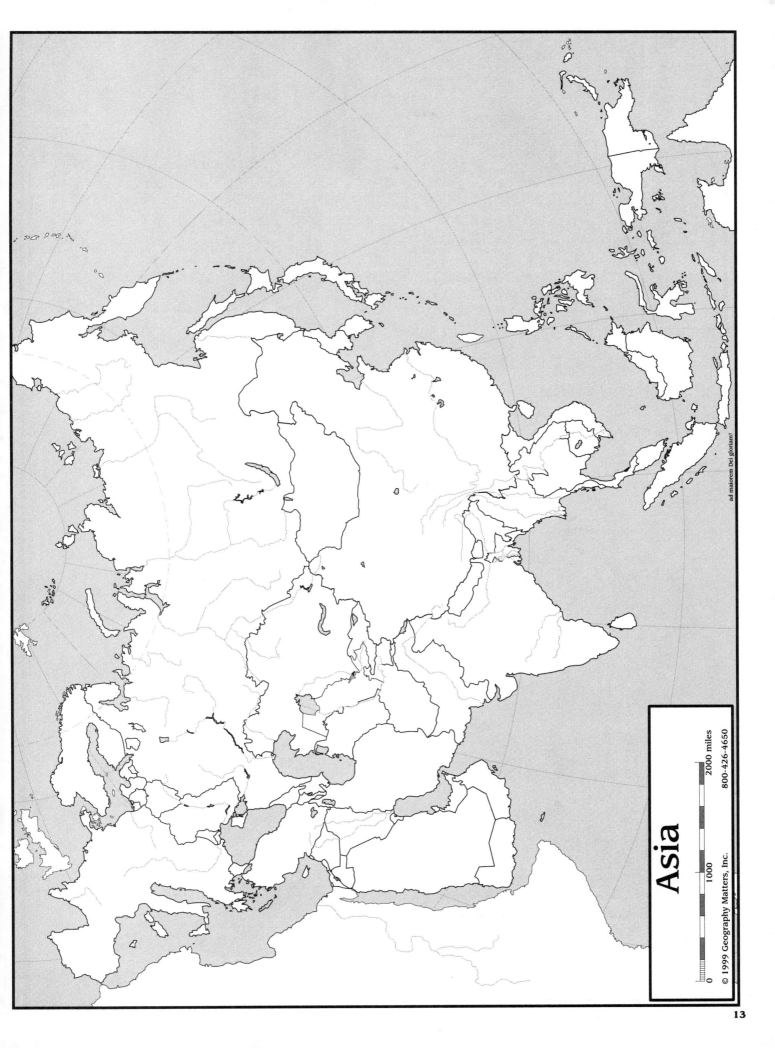

Asia

© 1999 Geography Matters, Inc.

0   1000   2000 miles

800-426-4650

ad maiorem Dei gloriam!

13

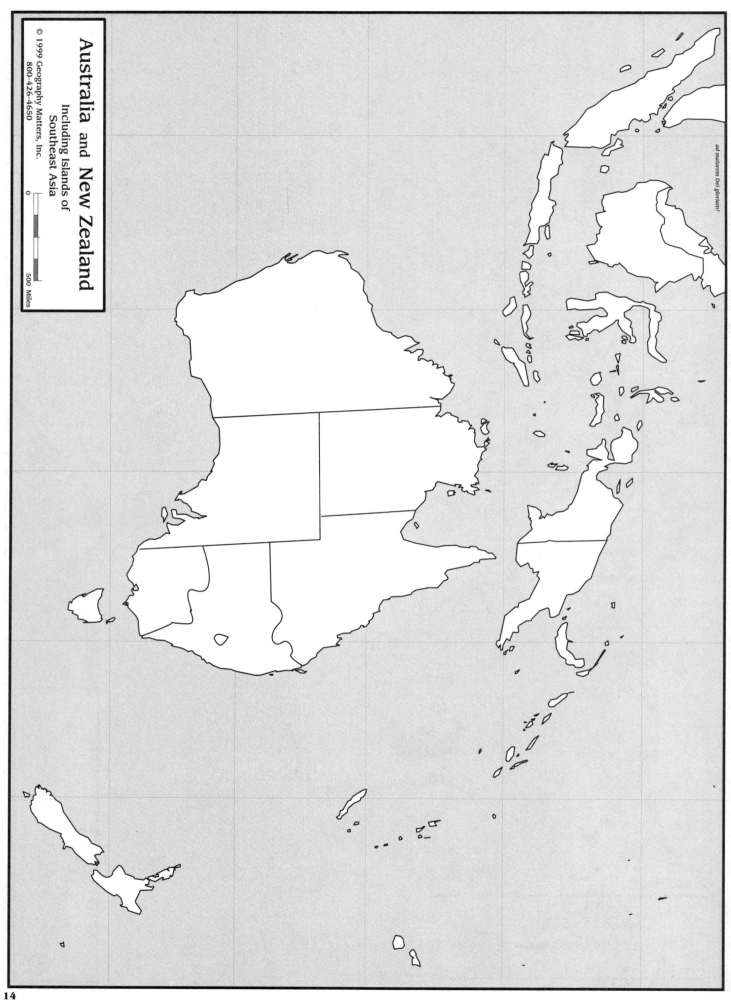

Australia and New Zealand
Including Islands of Southeast Asia

© 1999 Geography Matters, Inc.
800-426-4650

0   500 Miles

ad maiorem Dei gloriam!

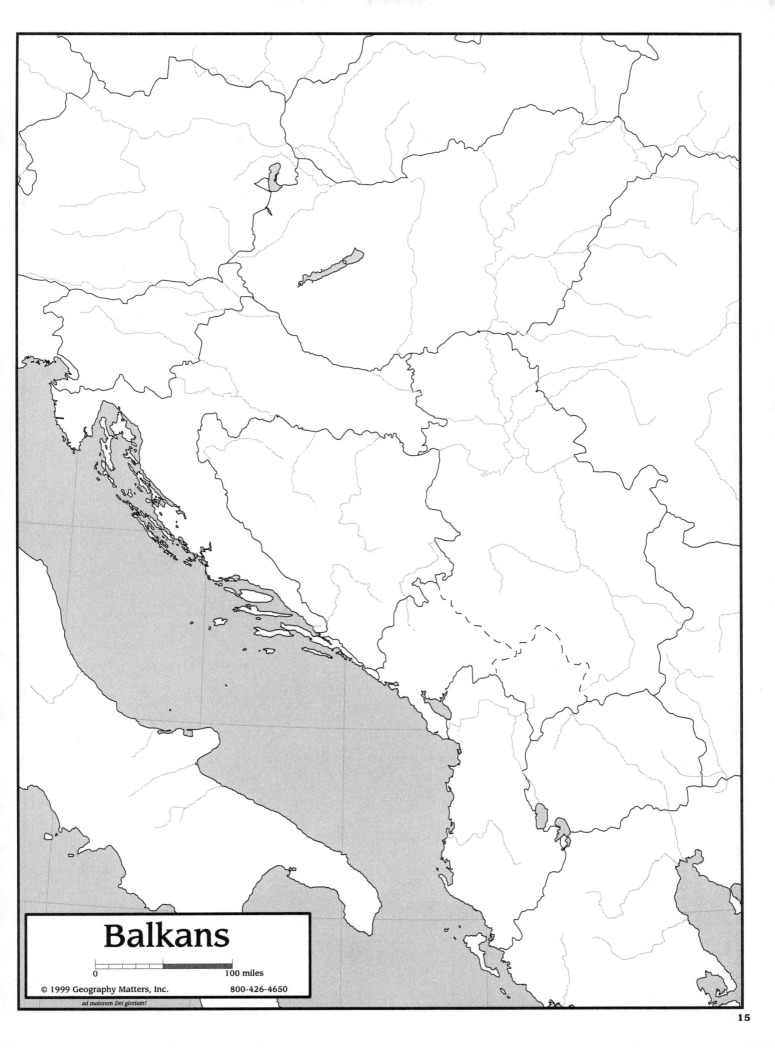

Balkans

0   100 miles

© 1999 Geography Matters, Inc.   800-426-4650

ad maiorem Dei gloriam!

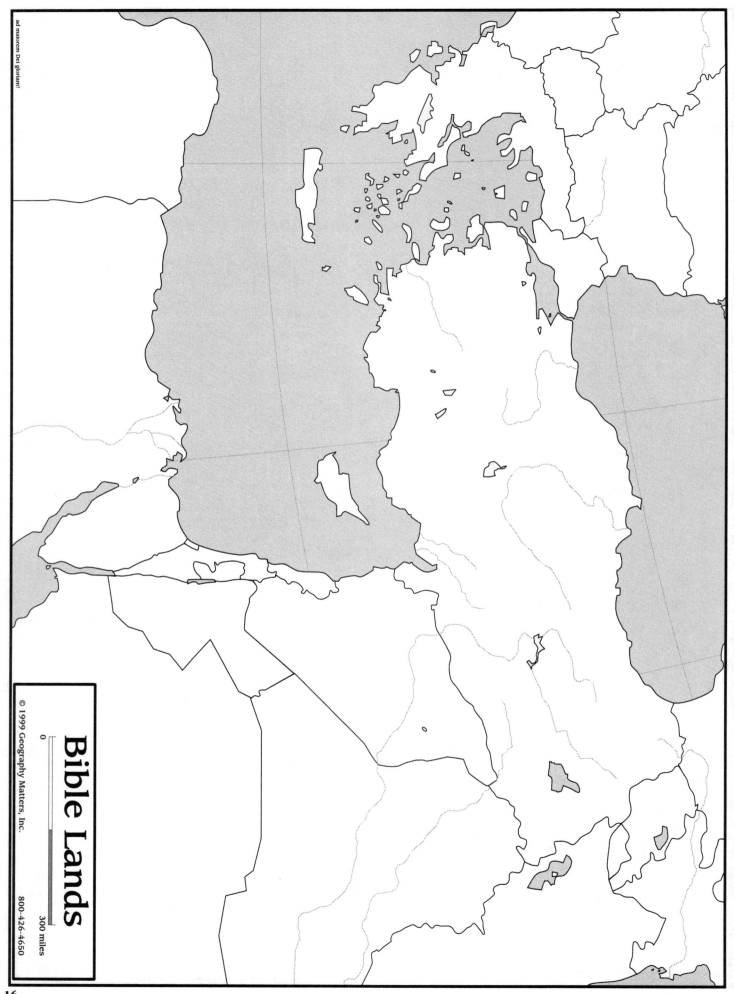

Bible Lands

800-426-4650

0

300 miles

Brazil

ad maiorem Dei gloriam!

0 500 miles

© 1999 Geography Matters, Inc.   800-426-4650

17

British Isles

0   50   100 miles

© 1999 Geography Matters, Inc.   800-426-4650

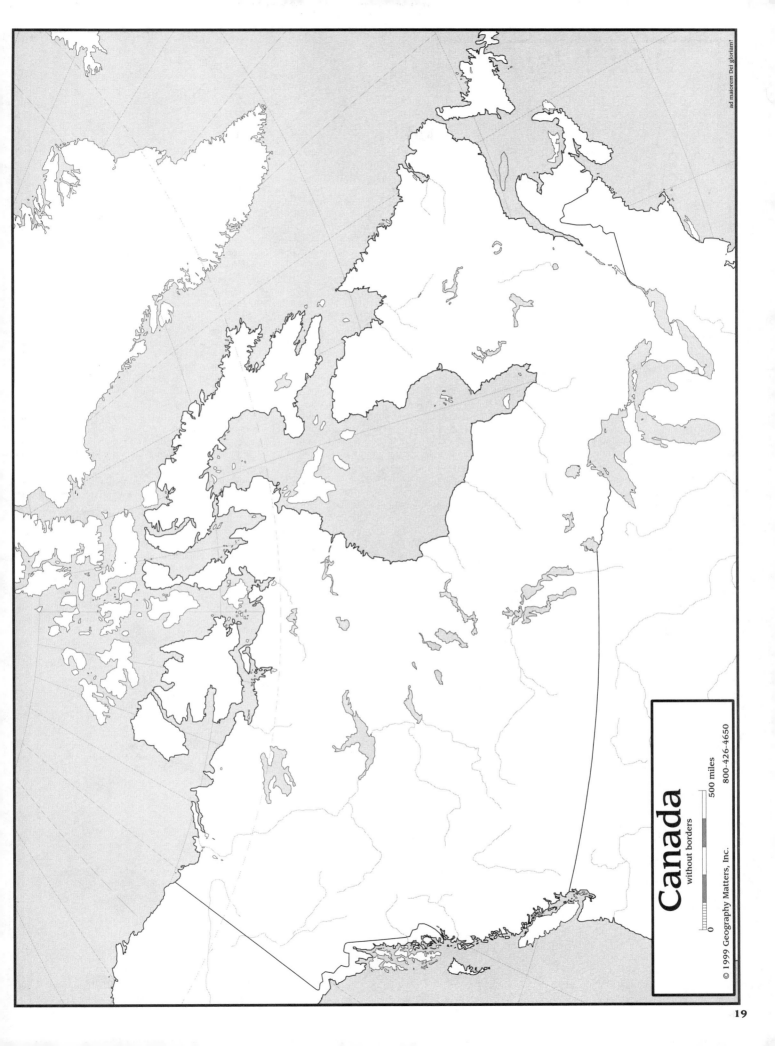

Canada
without borders

0 ___ 500 miles

© 1999 Geography Matters, Inc.

800-426-4650

ad maiorem Dei gloriam!

19

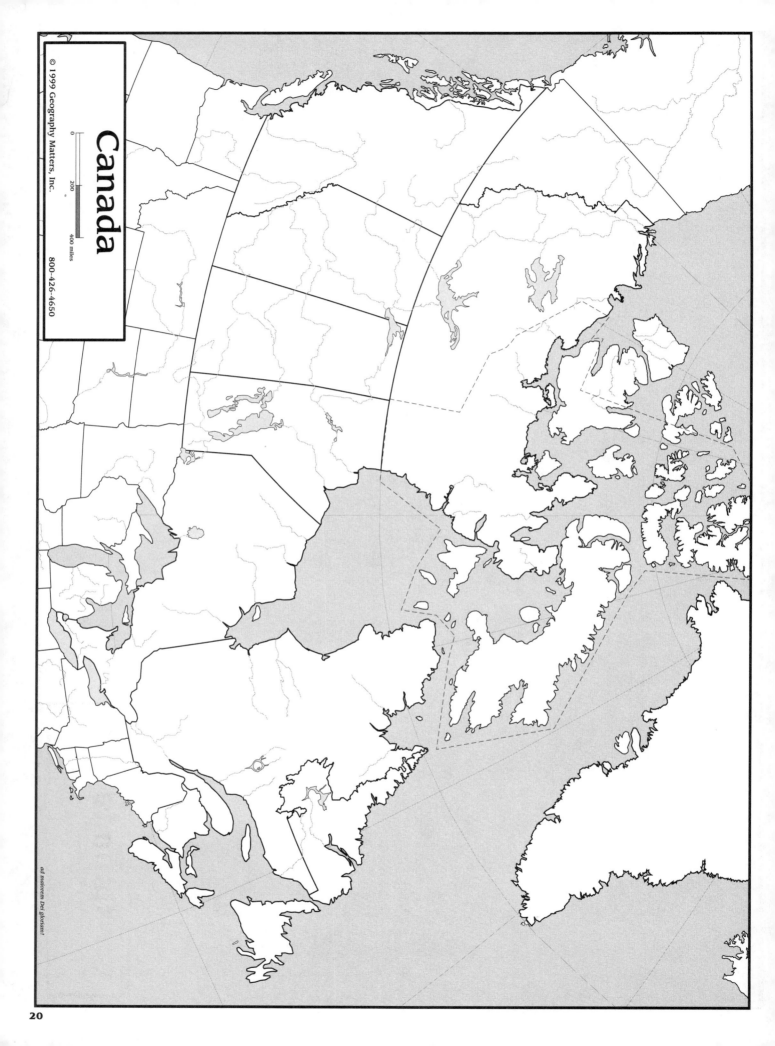

Canada

0 200 400 miles

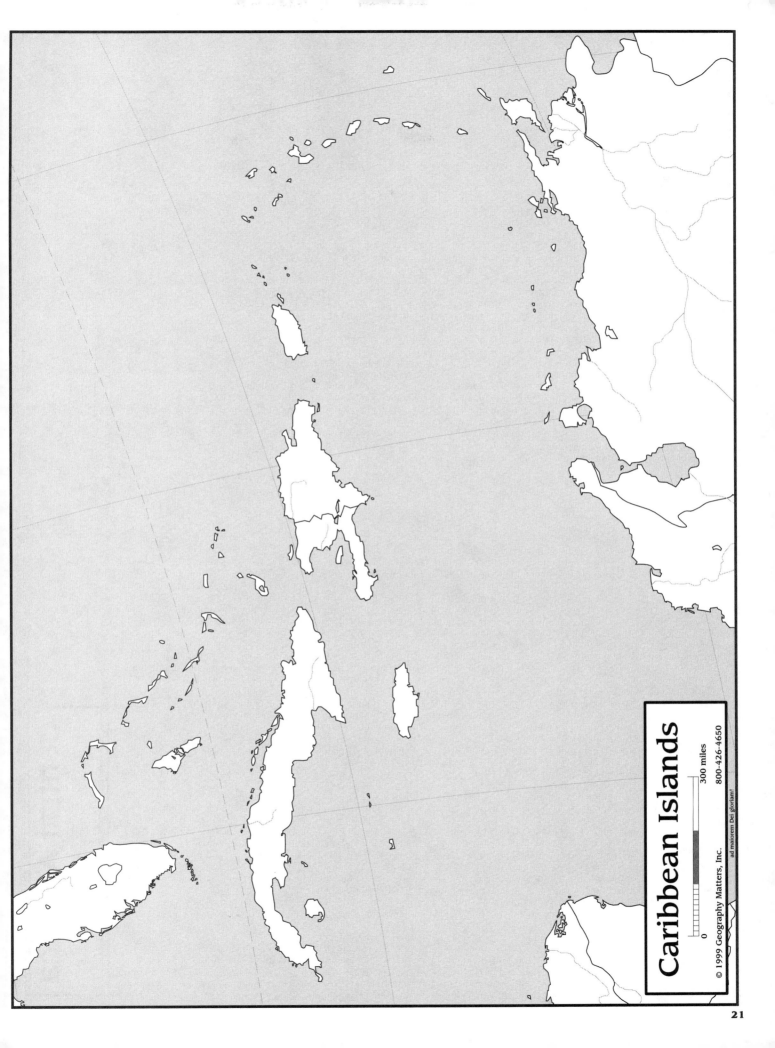

Caribbean Islands

0   300 miles

© 1999 Geography Matters, Inc.   800-426-4650

ad maiorem Dei gloriam!

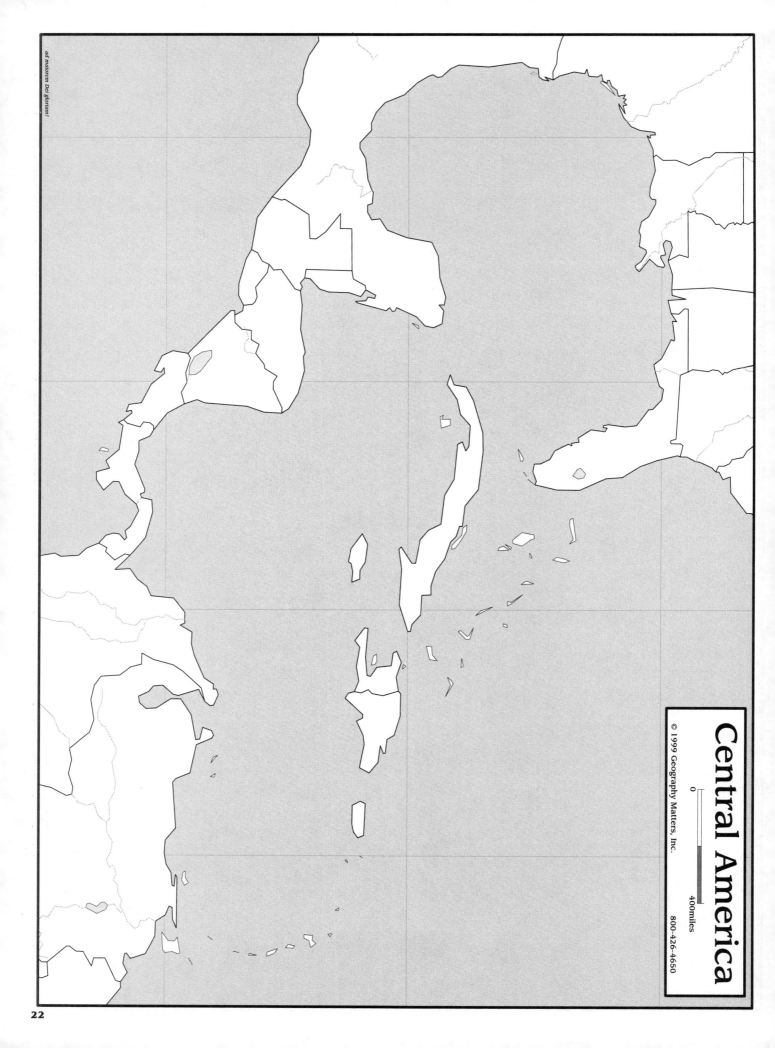

Central America

© 1999 Geography Matters, Inc.

800-426-4650

0　400miles

China and Mongolia

© 1999 Geography Matters, Inc.

800-426-4650

0 ▮▮▮▮▮▮▮ ▮ 1000 miles

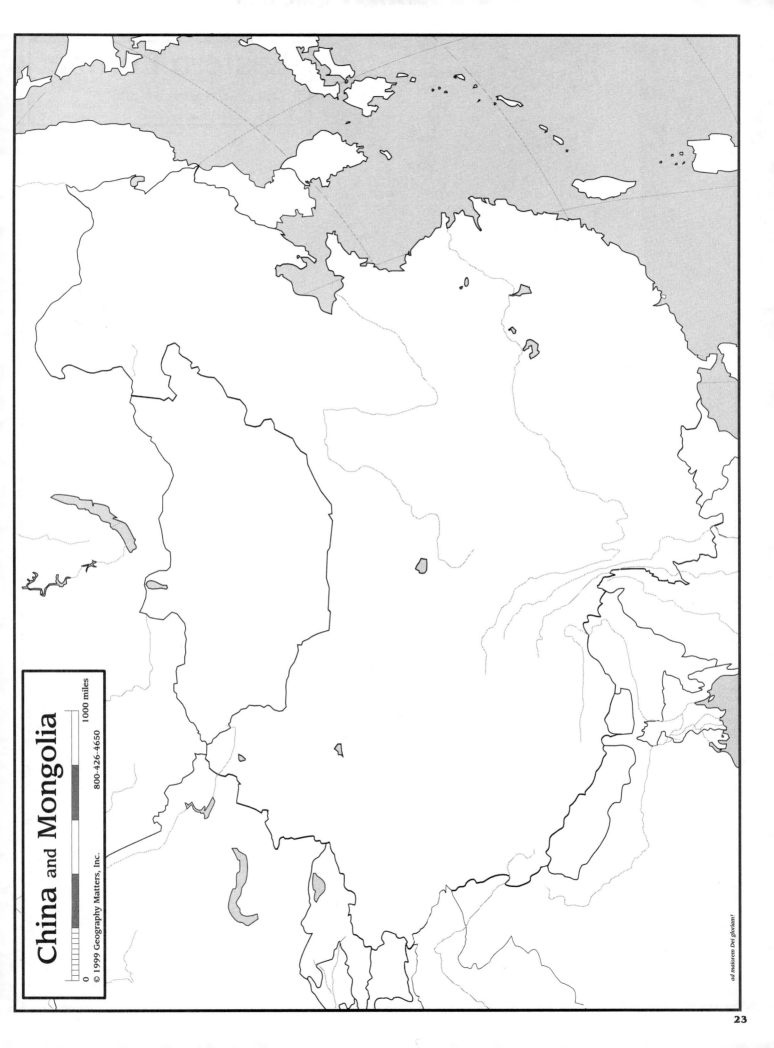

ad maiorem Dei gloriam!

0

300 miles

© 1999 Geography Matters, Inc.

800-426-4650

ad maiorem Dei gloriam!

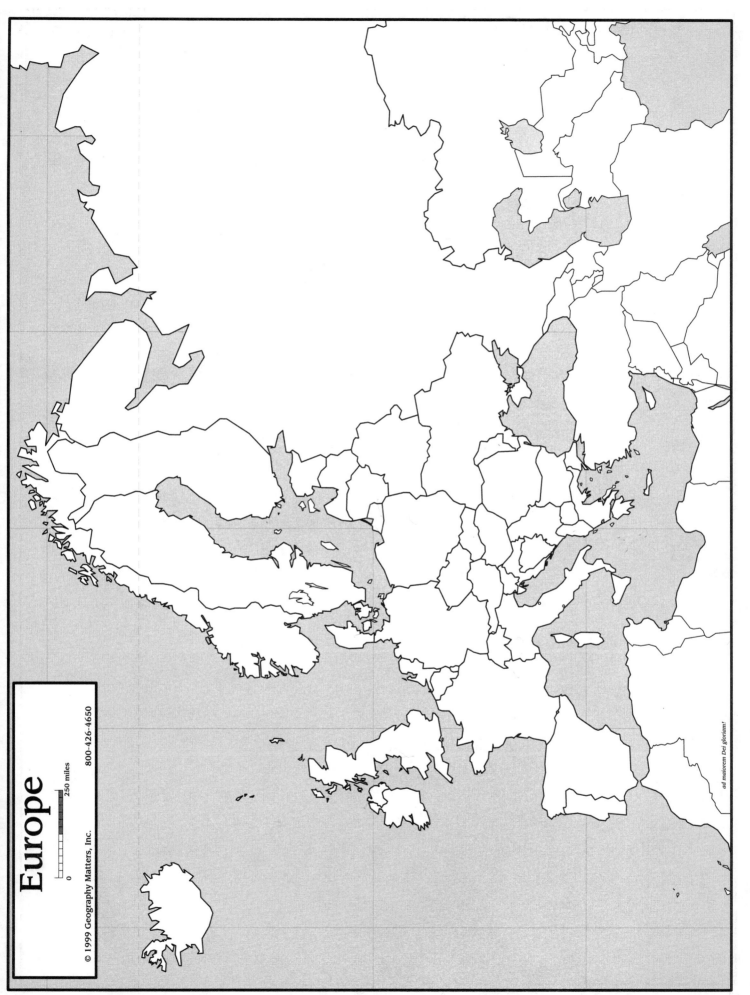

Europe

0 ___ 250 miles

© 1999 Geography Matters, Inc.

800-426-4650

ad maiorem Dei gloriam!

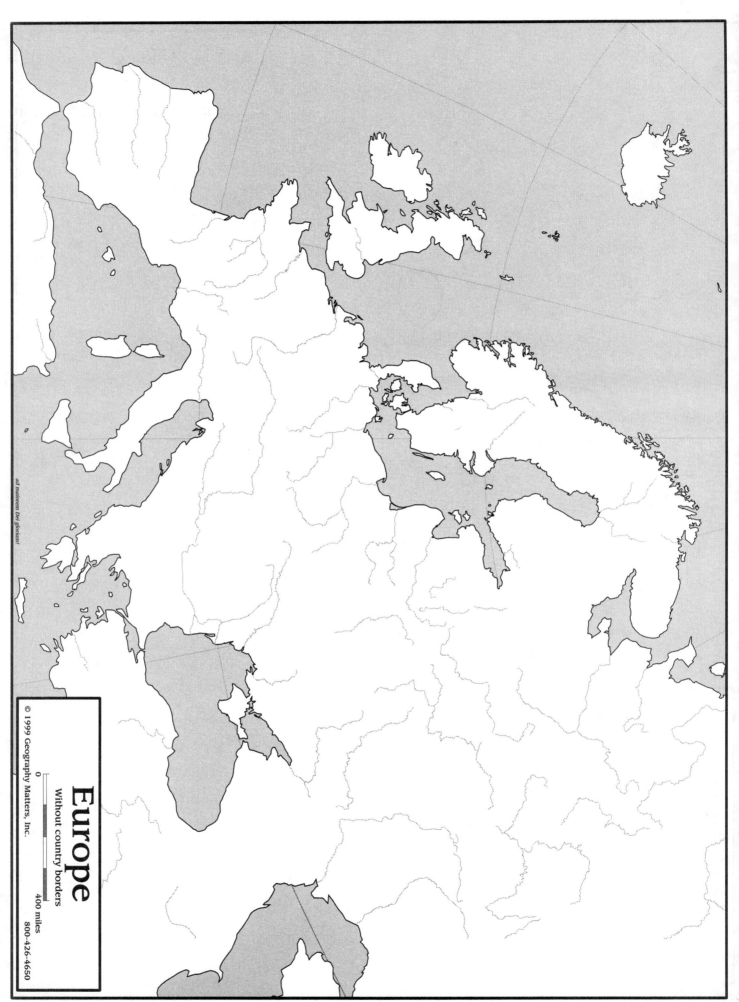

Europe

without country borders

ad maiorem Dei gloriam!

© 1999 Geography Matters, Inc.

0   400 miles

800-426-4650

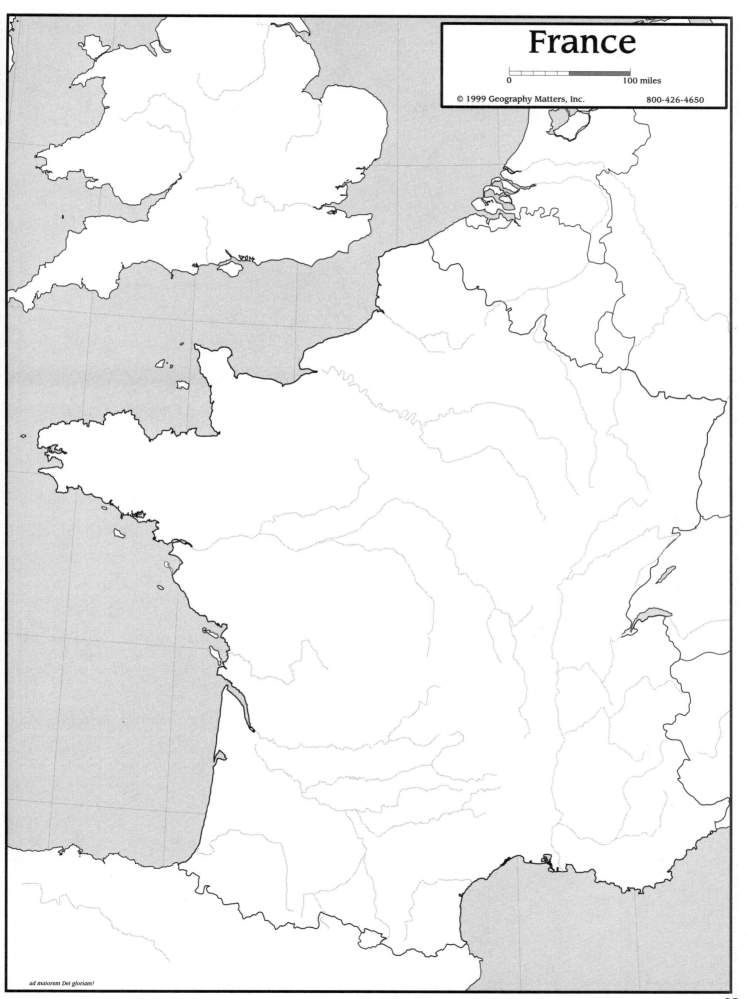

France

0 ——————————— 100 miles

© 1999 Geography Matters, Inc.   800-426-4650

ad maiorem Dei gloriam!

Germany

0   100 miles

© 1999 Geography Matters, Inc.   800-426-4650

ad maiorem Dei gloriam!

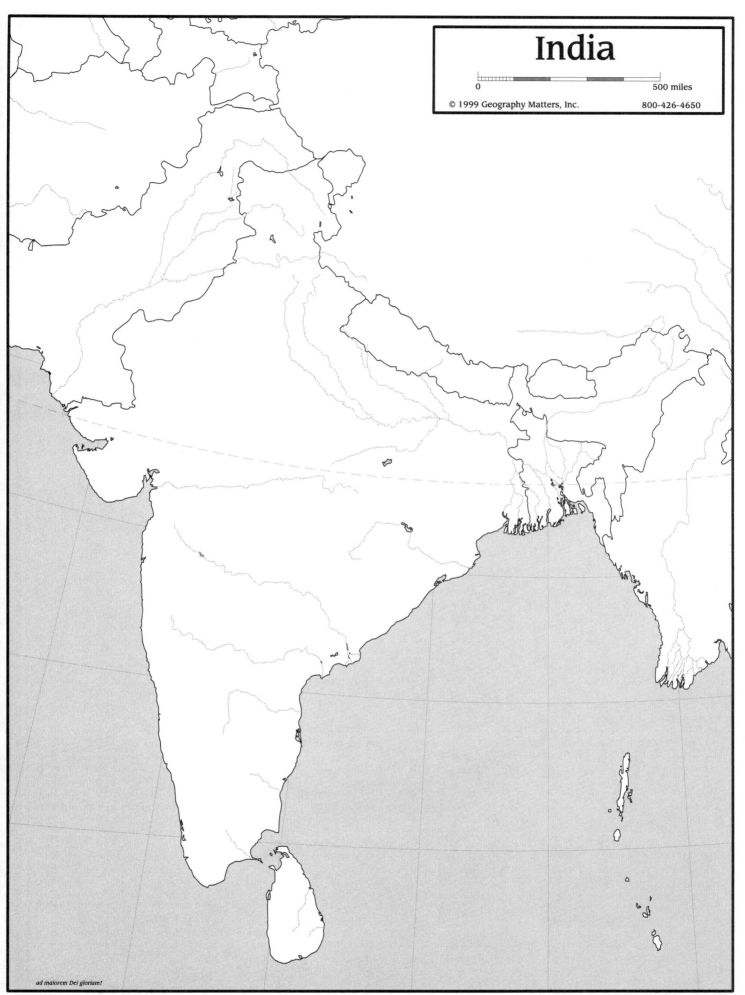

India

0 |▬▬▬▬▬▬▬▬▬| 500 miles

© 1999 Geography Matters, Inc.   800-426-4650

ad maiorem Dei gloriam!

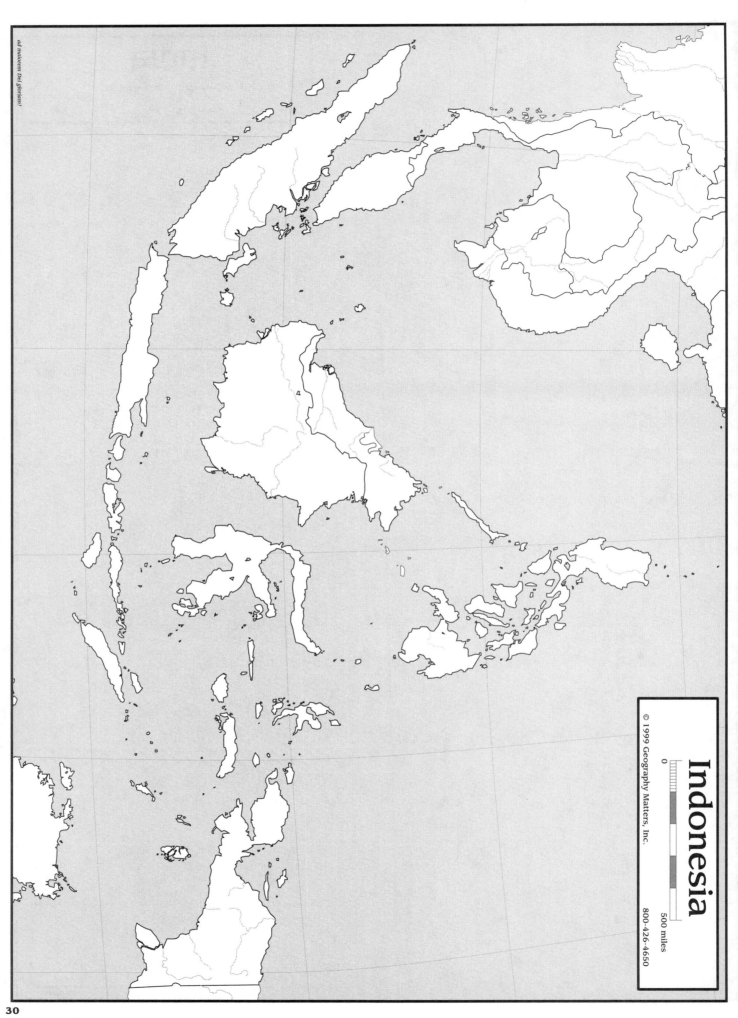

Indonesia

© 1999 Geography Matters, Inc.

0   500 miles

800-426-4650

ad maiorem Dei gloriam!

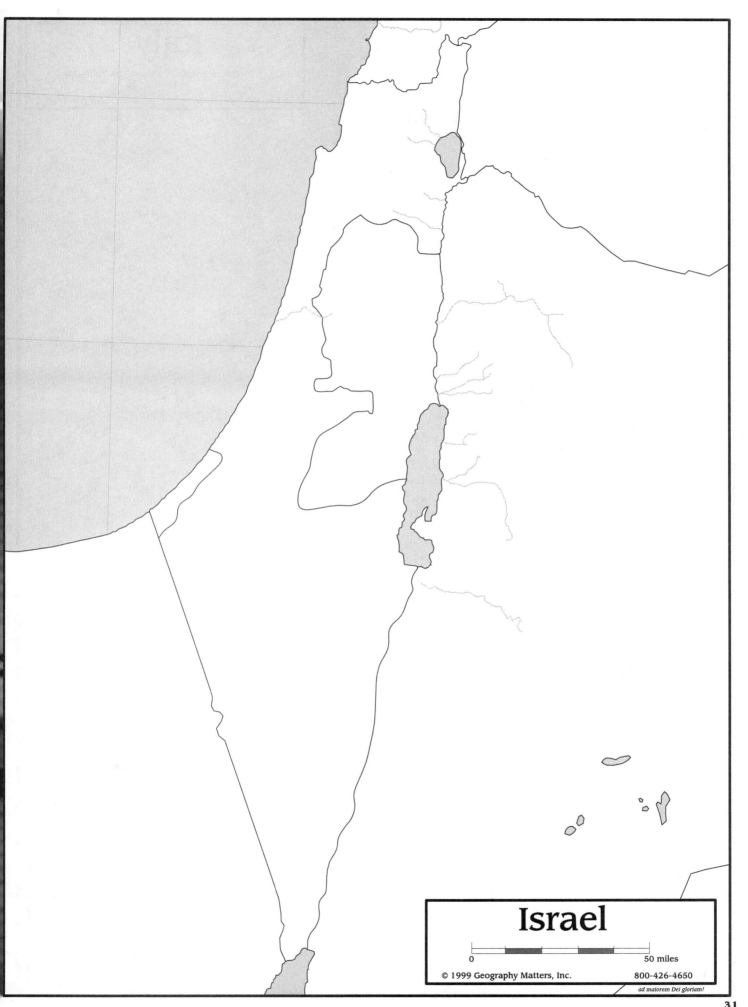

Israel

0 ▮▮▮▮▮▮ 50 miles

© 1999 Geography Matters, Inc.   800-426-4650

ad maiorem Dei gloriam!

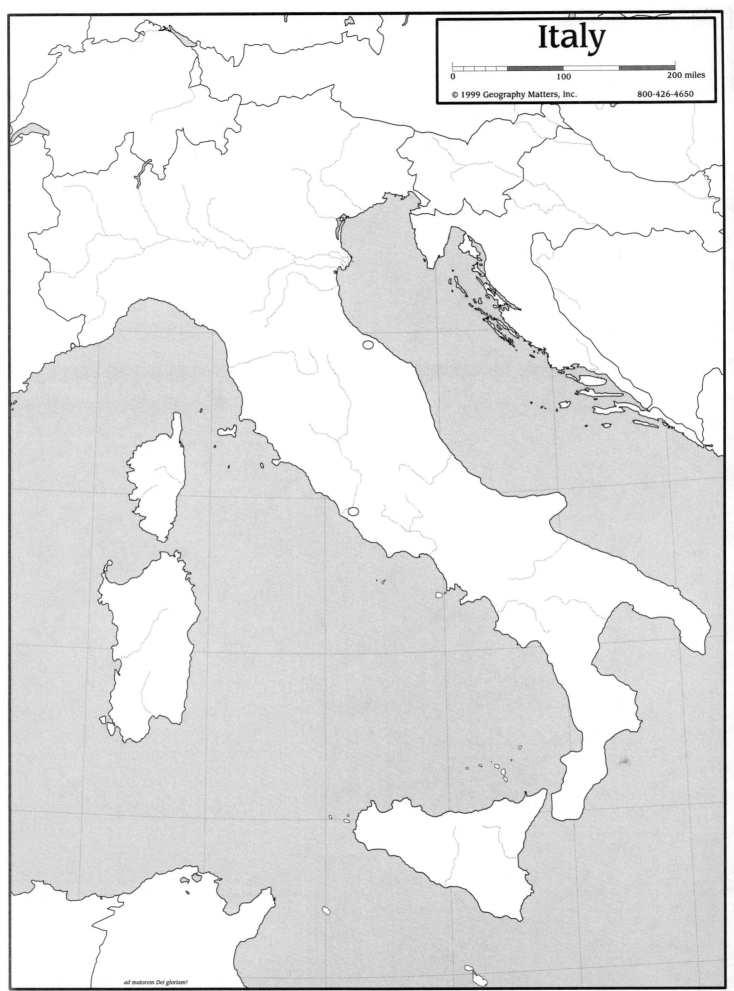

Italy

0   100   200 miles

© 1999 Geography Matters, Inc.   800-426-4650

ad maiorem Dei gloriam!

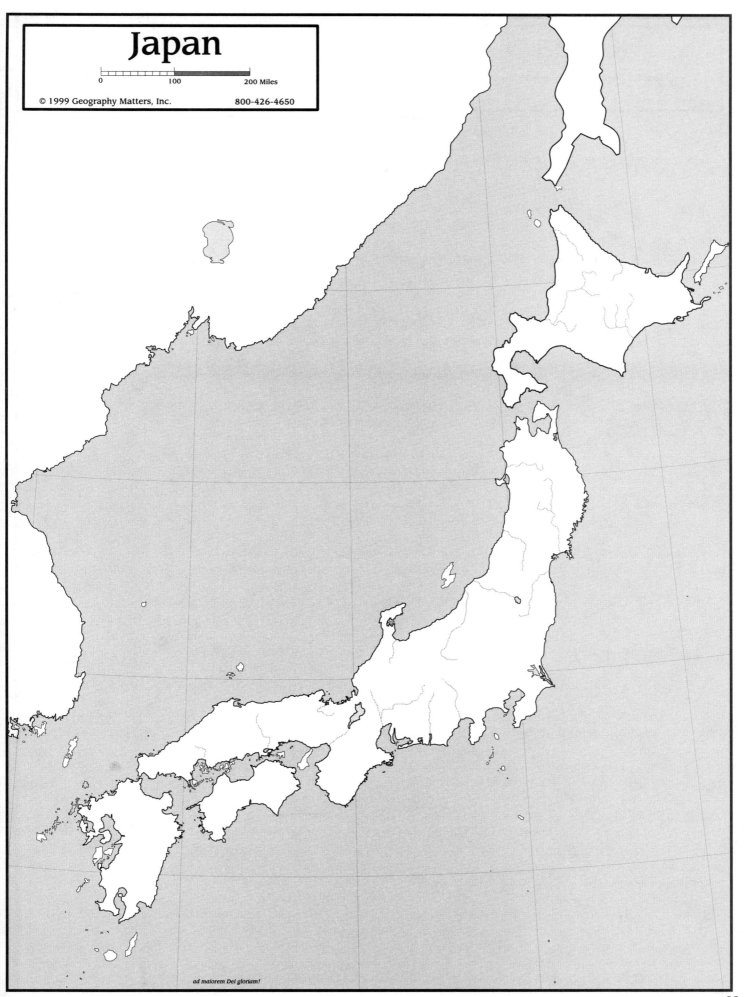

Japan

0   100   200 Miles

ad maiorem Dei gloriam!

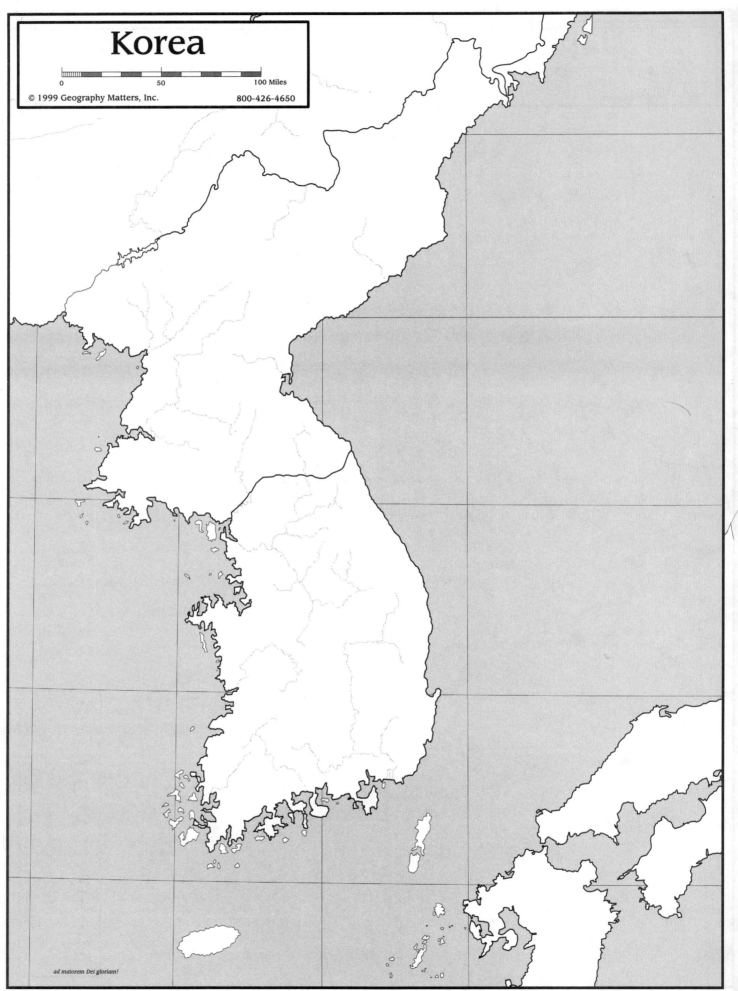

Korea

0   50   100 Miles

© 1999 Geography Matters, Inc.   800-426-4650

ad maiorem Dei gloriam!

34

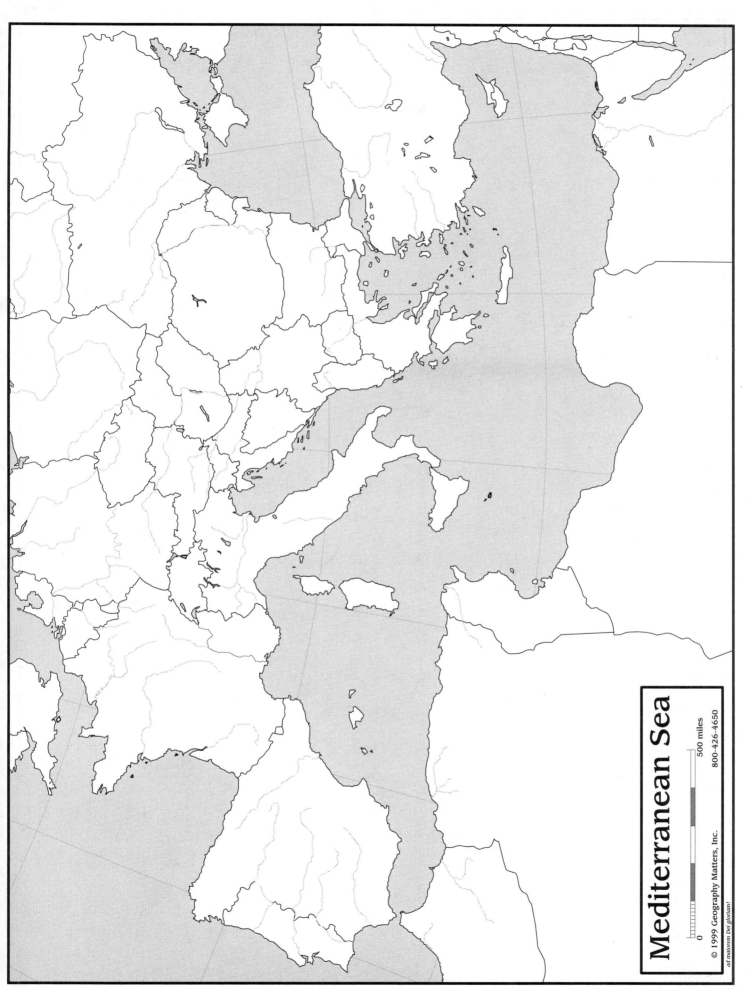

Mediterranean Sea

0 500 miles

© 1999 Geography Matters, Inc.

800-426-4650

ad maiorem Dei gloriam!

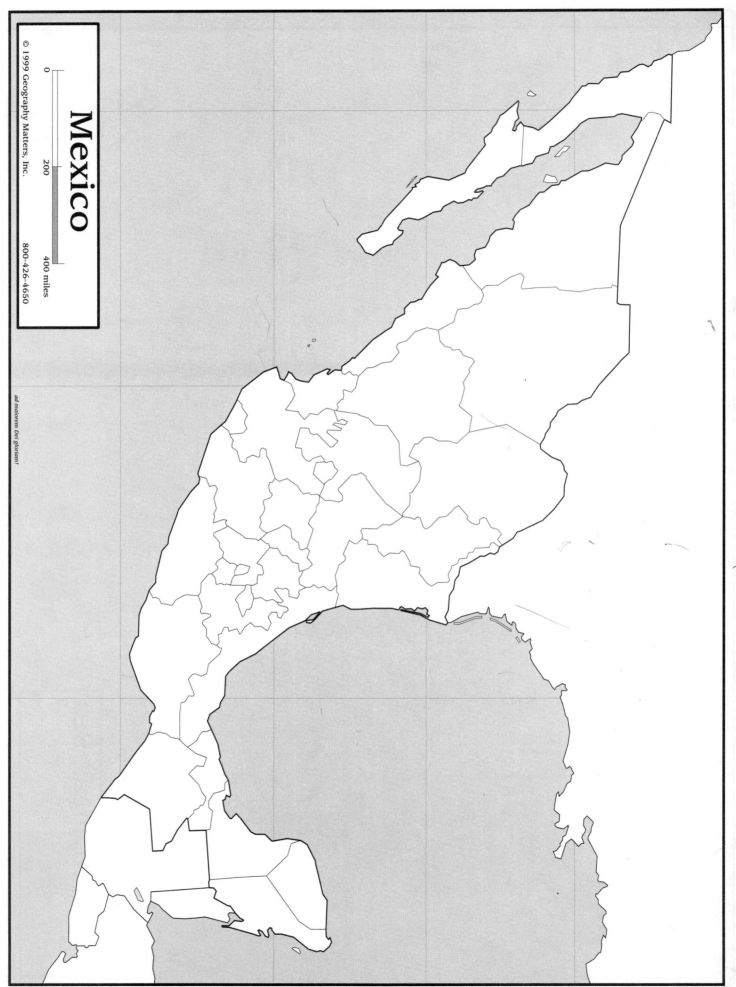

Mexico

0   200   400 miles

ad maiorem Dei gloriam!

36

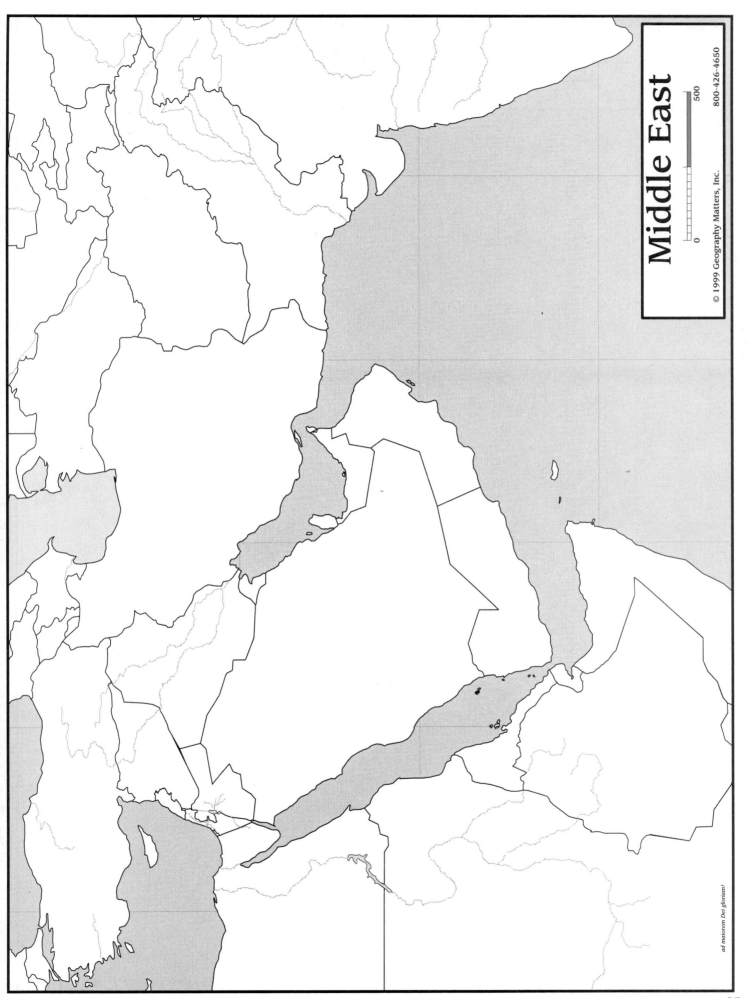

Middle East

© 1999 Geography Matters, Inc.

0   500

800-426-4650

ad maiorem Dei gloriam!

Netherlands
Belgium and Luxembourg

0   100 miles

© 1999 Geography Matters, Inc.   800-426-4650

N

ad maiorem Dei gloriam!

North America

0   750   1500 miles

© 1999 Geography Matters, Inc.   800-426-4650

ad maiorem Dei gloriam!

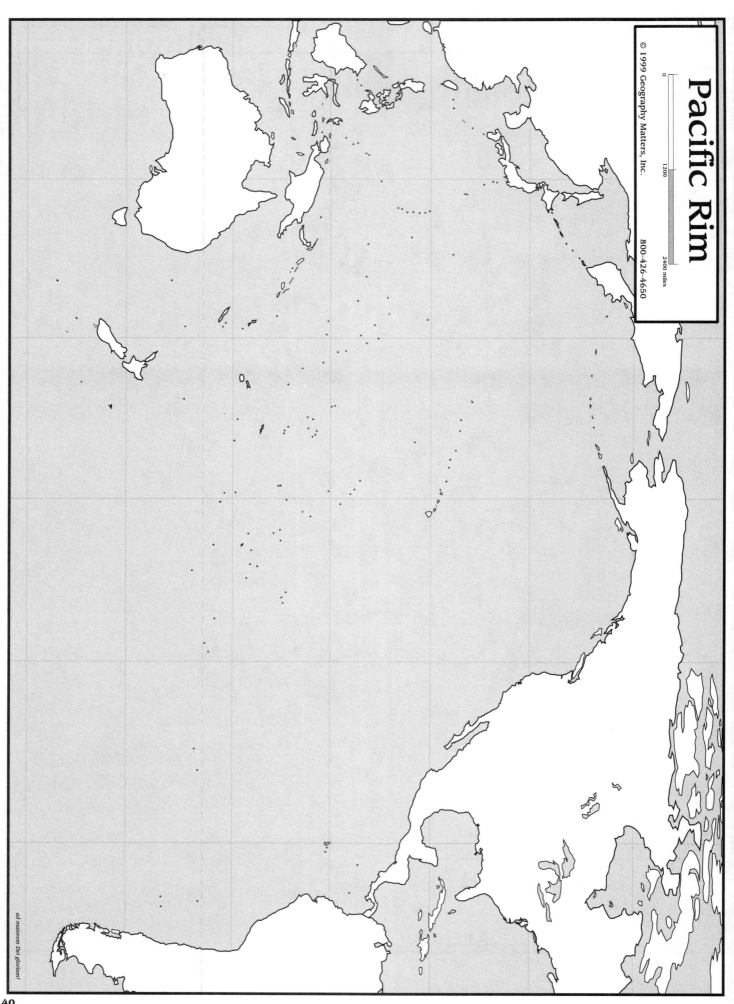

Pacific Rim

800-426-4650

0   1200   2400 miles

ad maiorem Dei gloriam!

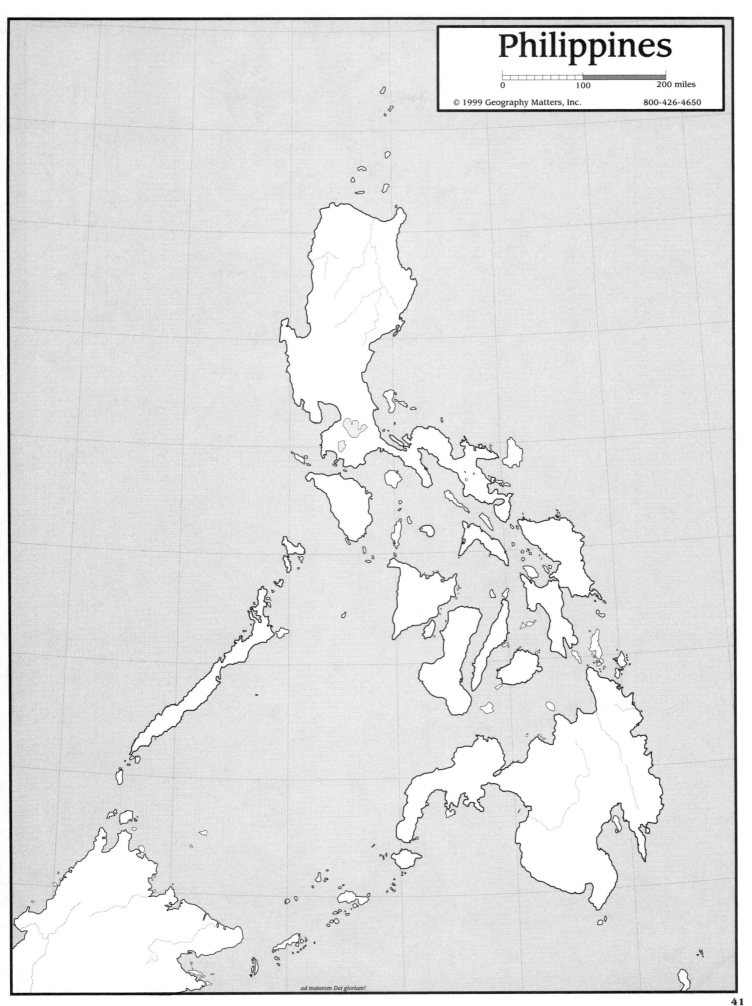

Philippines

0   100   200 miles

ad maiorem Dei gloriam!

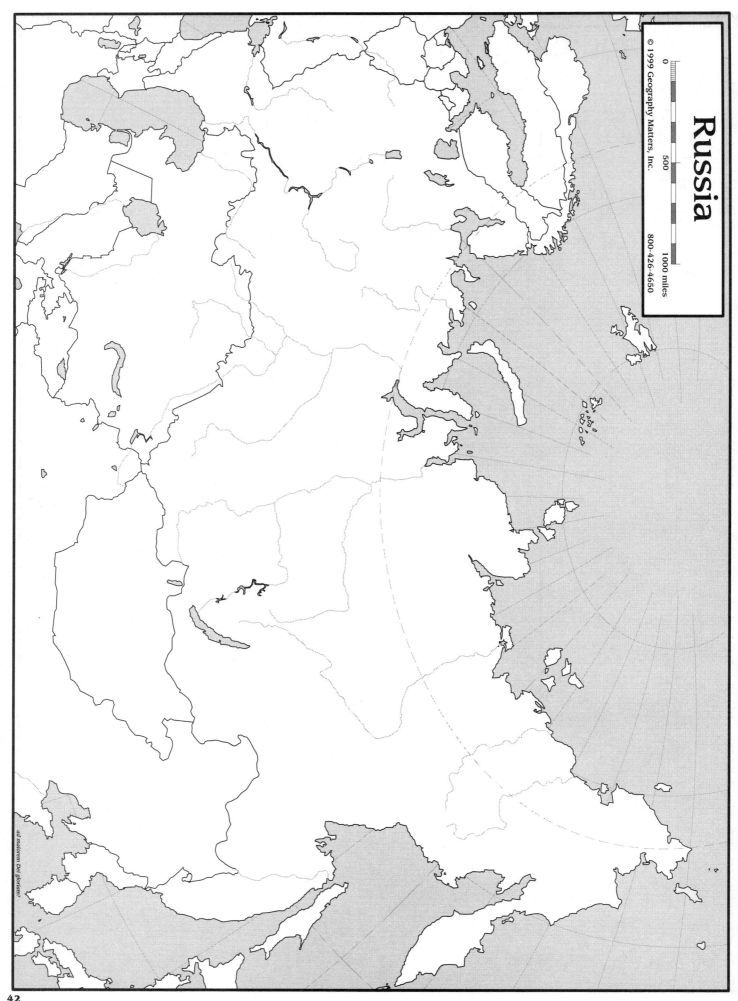

Russia

0   500   1000 miles

800-426-4650

ad maiorem Dei gloriam!

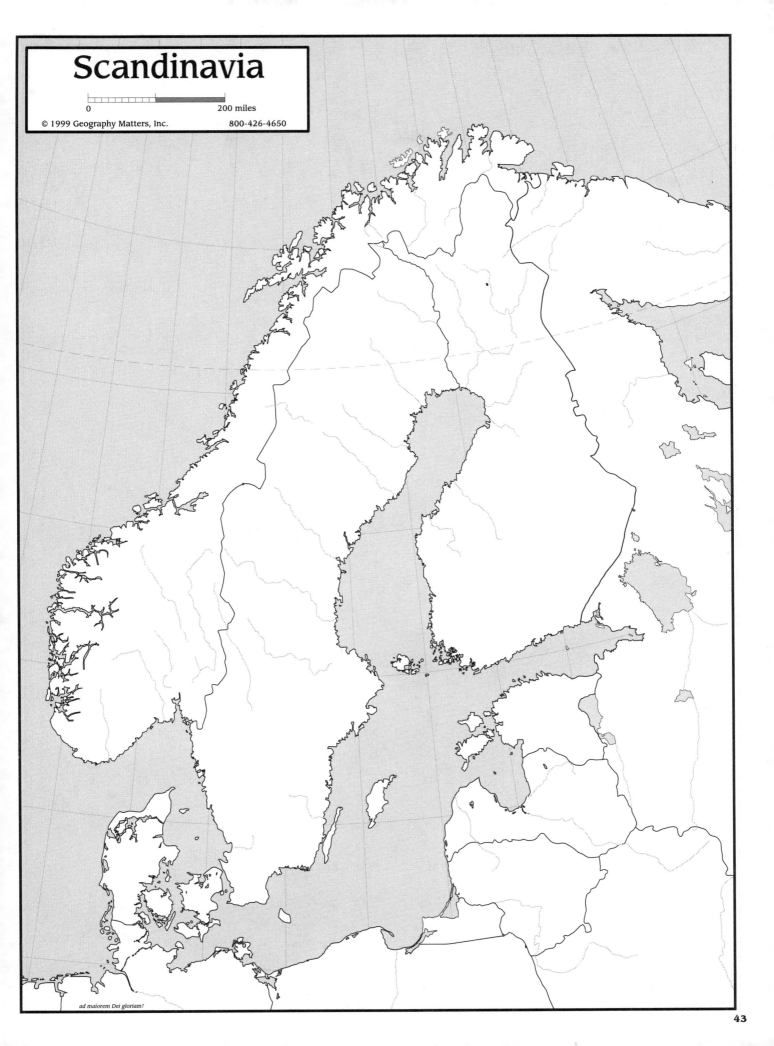

Scandinavia

0   200 miles

© 1999 Geography Matters, Inc.   800-426-4650

ad maiorem Dei gloriam!

43

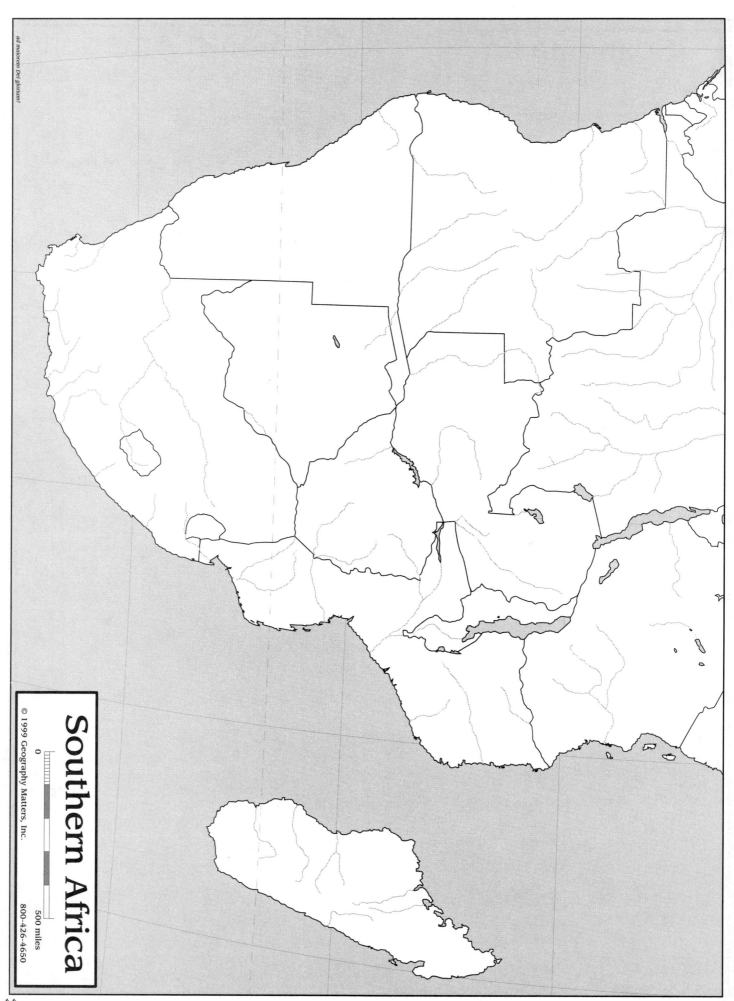

Southern Africa

0

500 miles

South America

0   600   1200 miles

© 1999 Geography Matters, Inc.   800-426-4650

ad maiorem Dei gloriam!

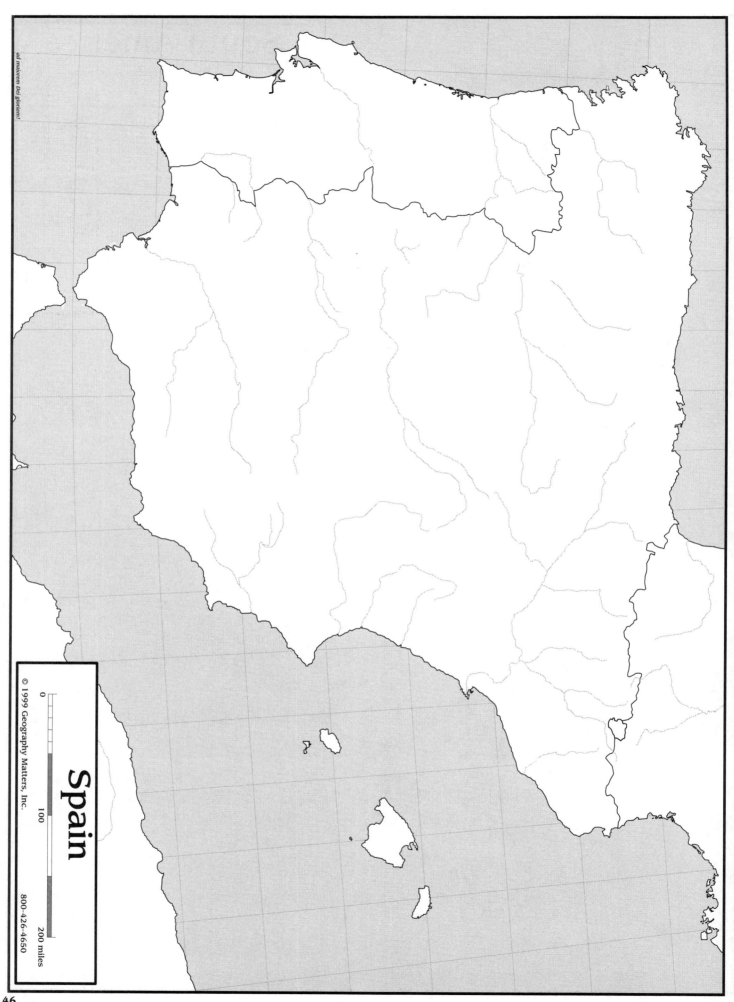

© 1999 Geography Matters, Inc.

800-426-4650

Spain

0

100

200 miles

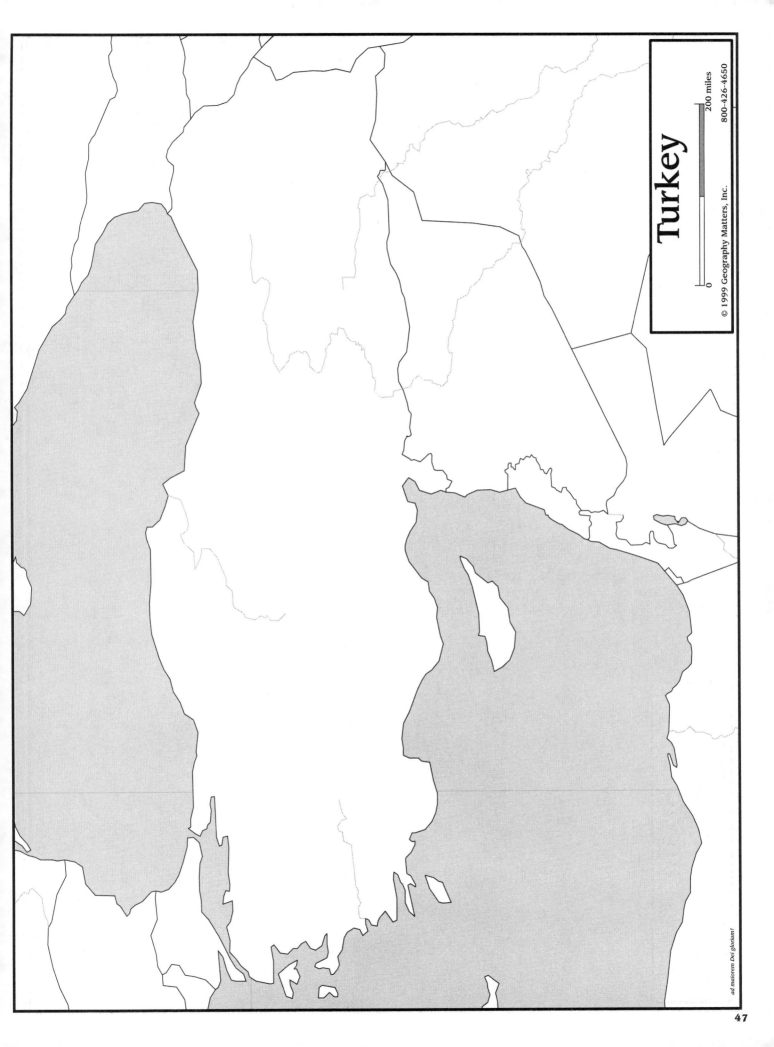

Turkey

0   200 miles

© 1999 Geography Matters, Inc.

800-426-4650

ad maiorem Dei gloriam!

47

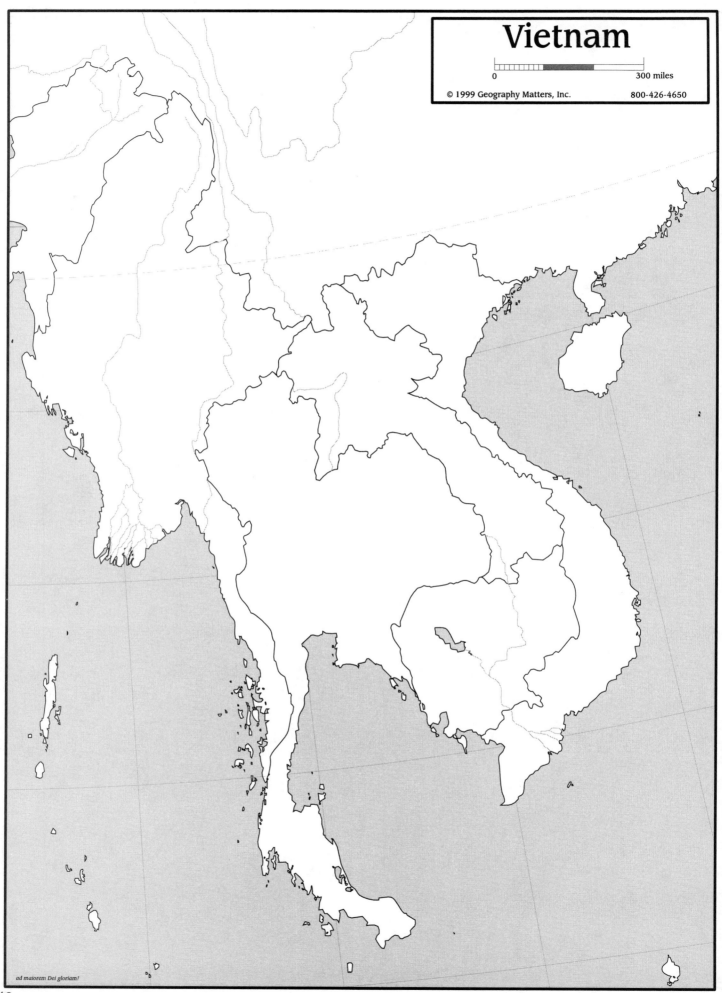

Vietnam

0   300 miles

© 1999 Geography Matters, Inc.   800-426-4650

ad maiorem Dei gloriam!

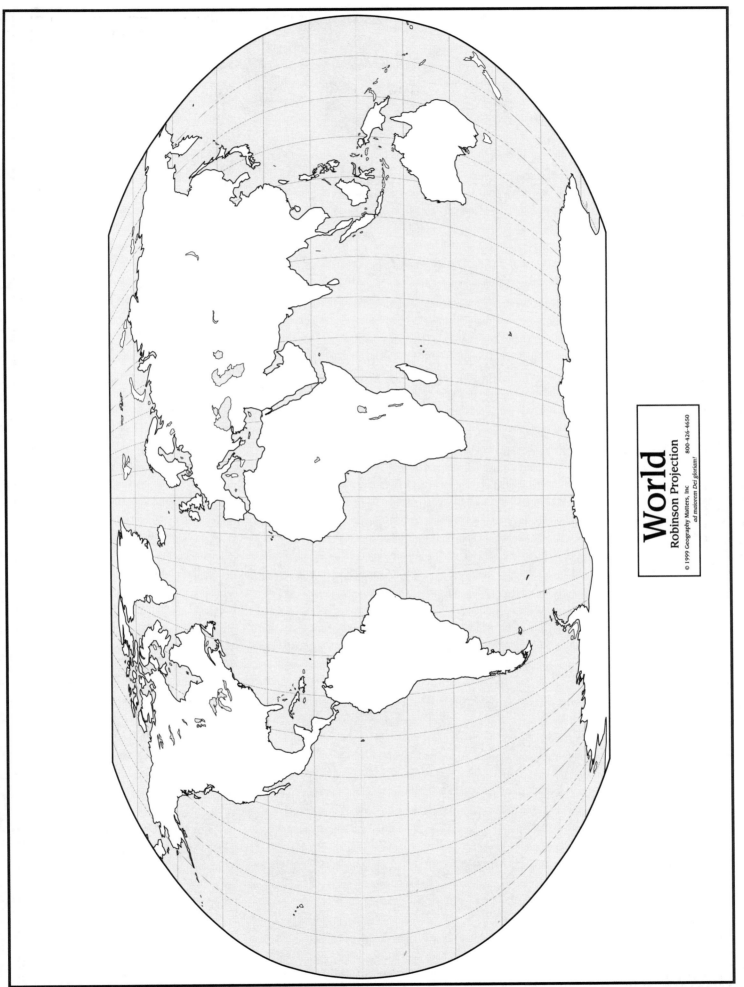

World
Robinson Projection
© 1999 Geography Matters, Inc   800-426-4650
ad maiorem Dei gloriam!

49

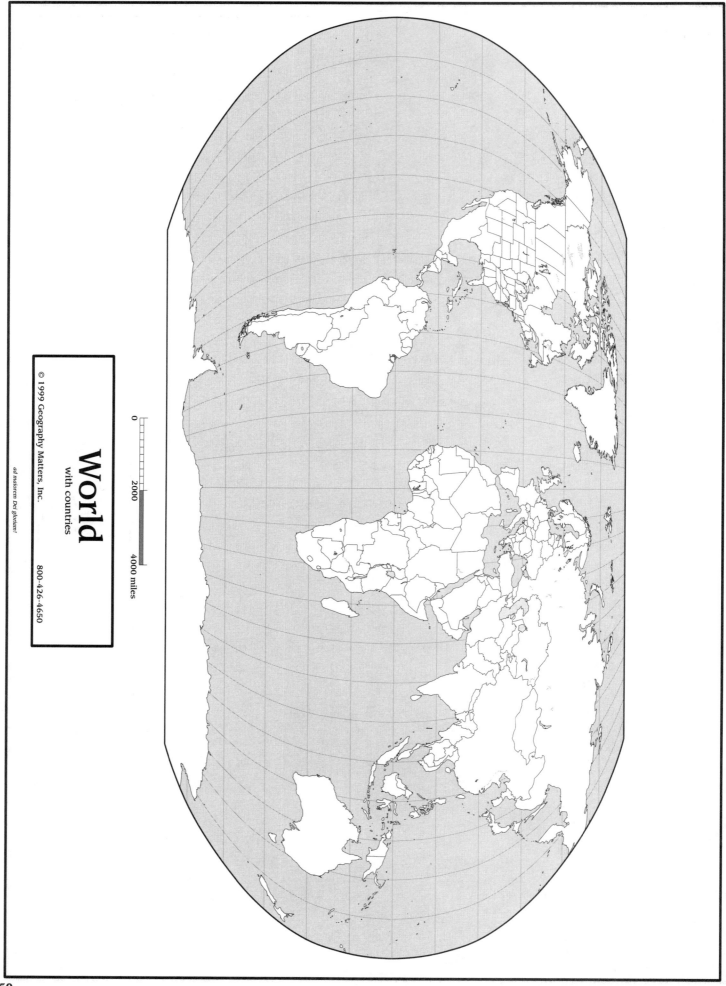

World
with countries

0 2000 4000 miles

© 1999 Geography Matters, Inc.   800-426-4650

ad maiorem Dei gloriam!

Eastern USA

0   175   350 miles

© 1999 Geography Matters, Inc.   800-426-4650

ad maiorem Dei gloriam!

51

Mid-Atlantic States

0   100 miles

ad maiorem Dei gloriam!

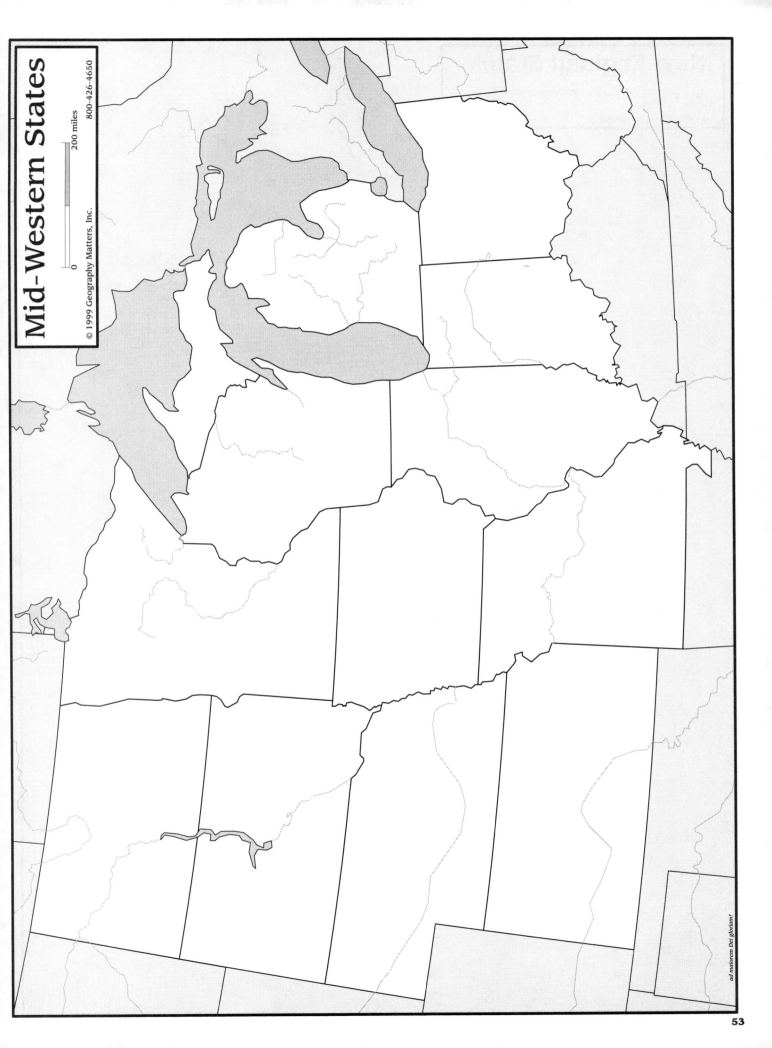

Mid-Western States

200 miles

0

© 1999 Geography Matters, Inc.

800-426-4650

ad maiorem Dei gloriam!

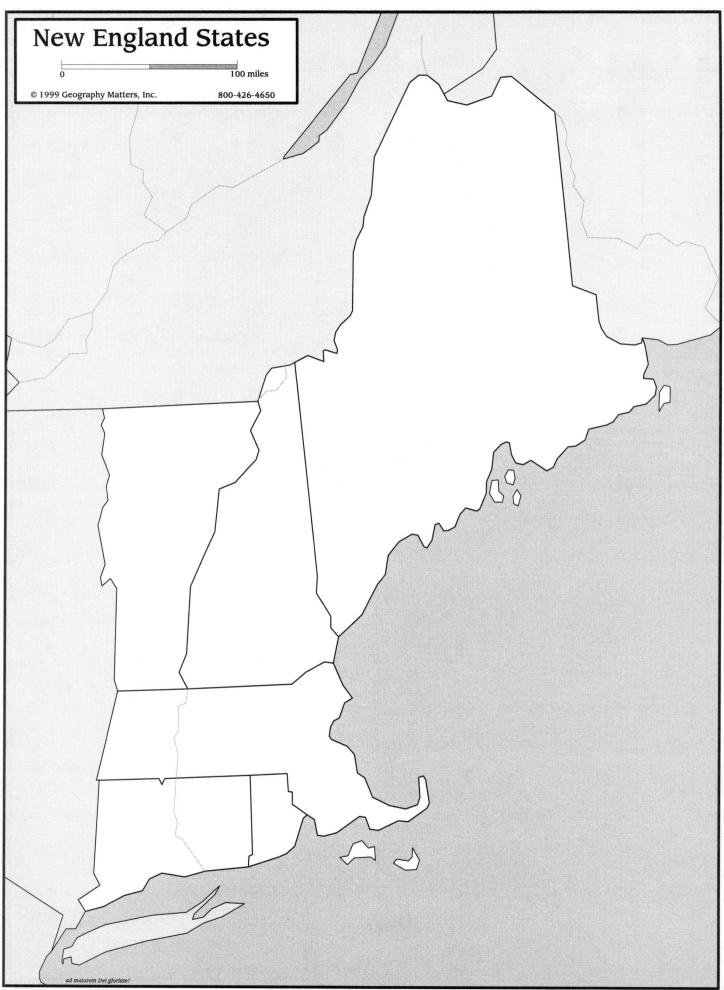

New England States

0   100 miles

© 1999 Geography Matters, Inc.   800-426-4650

ad maiorem Dei gloriam!

Pacific Coast States

0   100   200

© 1999 Geography Matters, Inc.   800-426-4650

ad maiorem Dei gloriam!

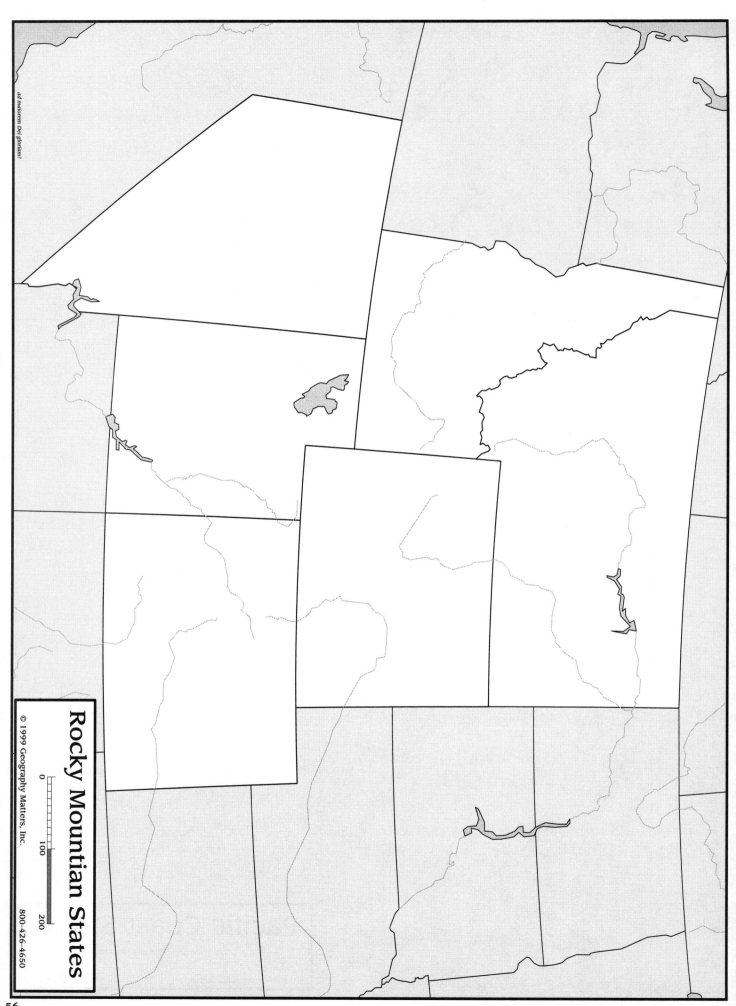

Rocky Mountian States

© 1999 Geography Matters, Inc.

0

100

200

800-426-4650

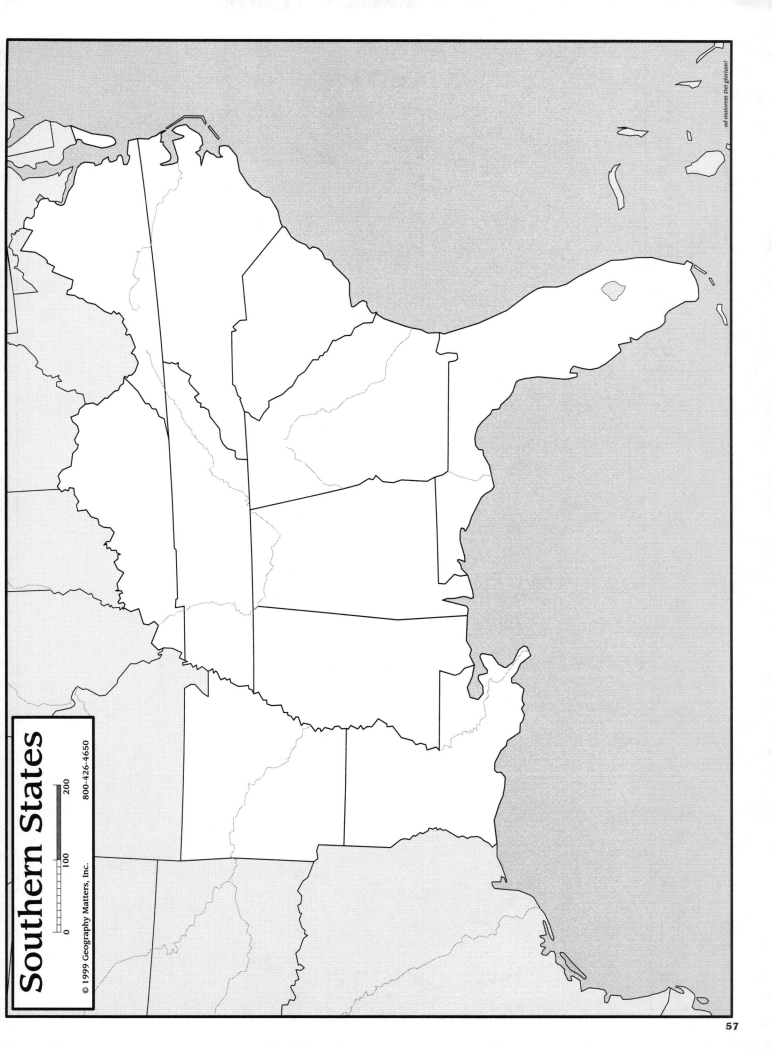

Southern States

© 1999 Geography Matters, Inc.   800-426-4650

0   100   200

ad maiorem Dei gloriam!

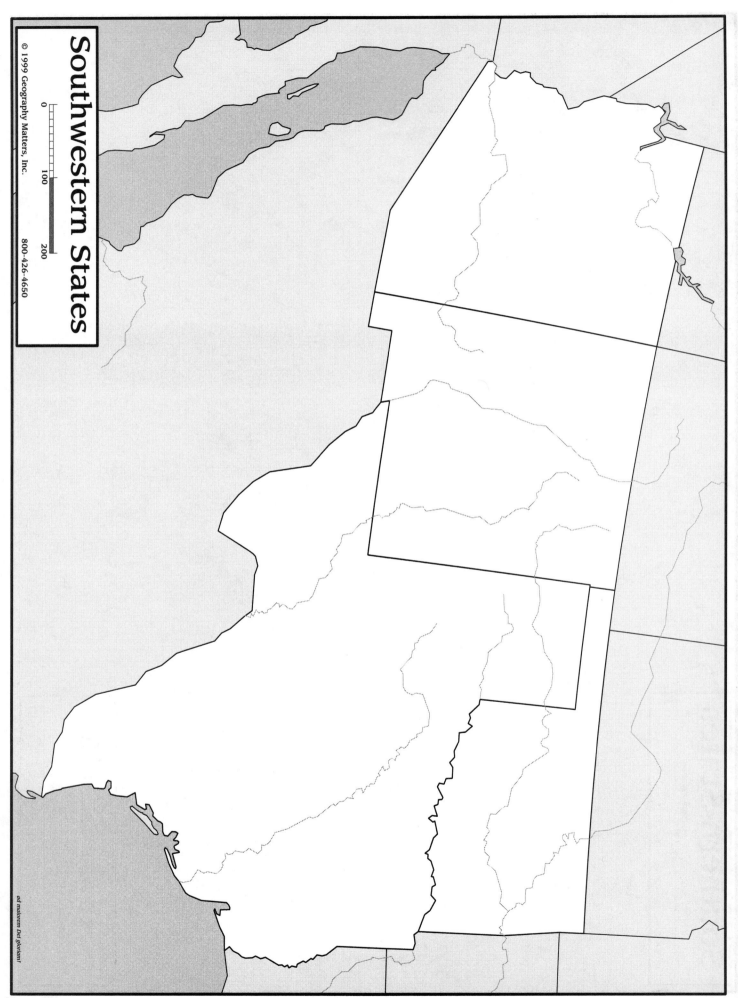

Southwestern States

0   100   200

800-426-4650

ad maiorem Dei gloriam

United States

without states

© 1999 Geography Matters, Inc.

0   100   200

800-426-4650

ad maiorem Dei gloriam!

59

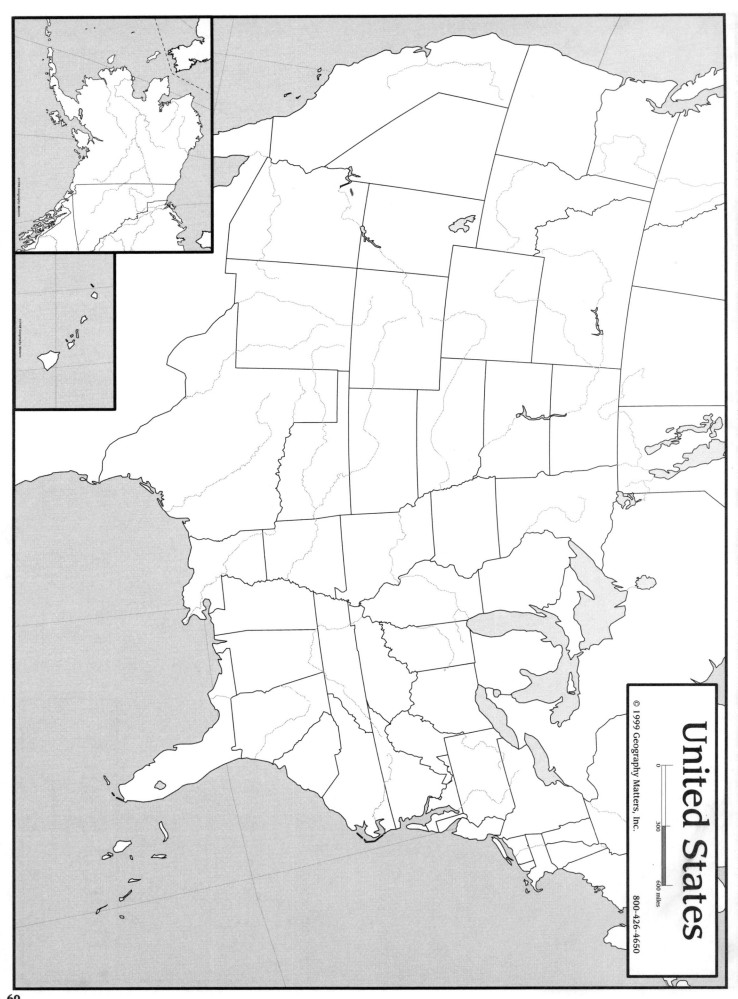

United States

0   300   600 miles

© 1999 Geography Matters, Inc.   800-426-4650

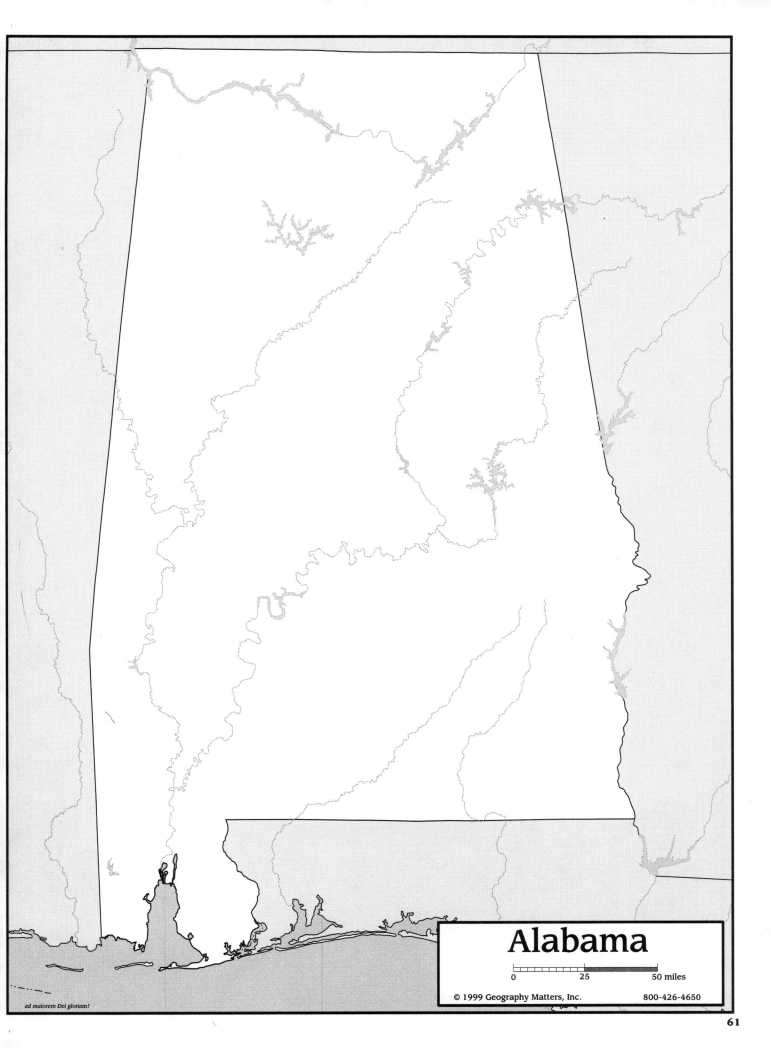

Alabama

0   25   50 miles

© 1999 Geography Matters, Inc.   800-426-4650

ad maiorem Dei gloriam!

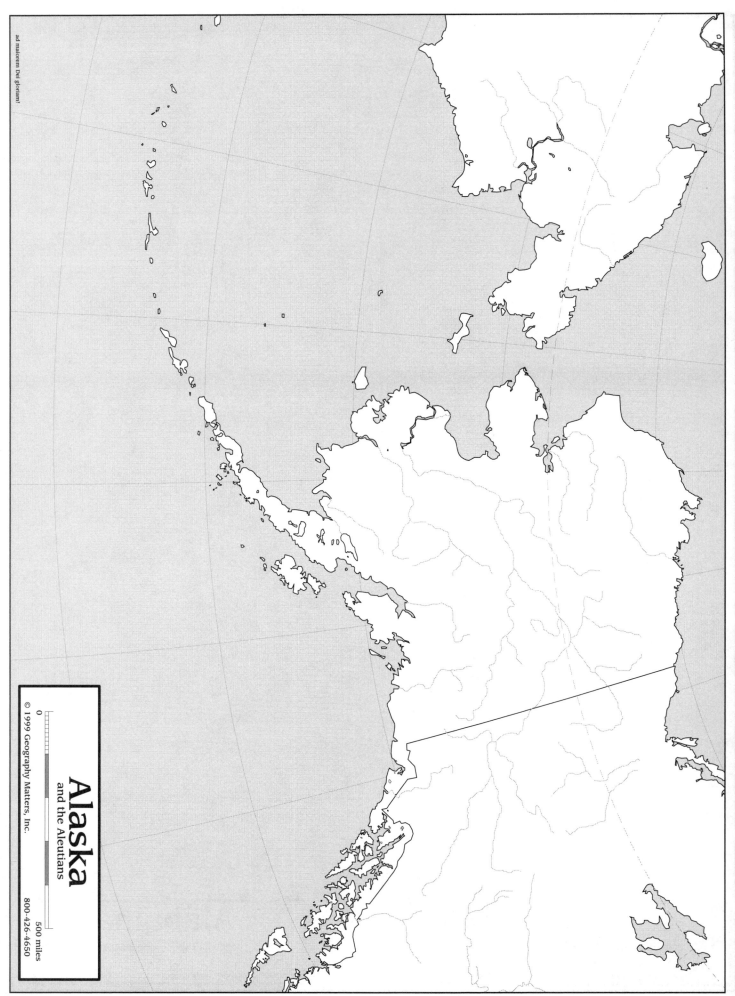

Alaska
and the Aleutians

0

500 miles

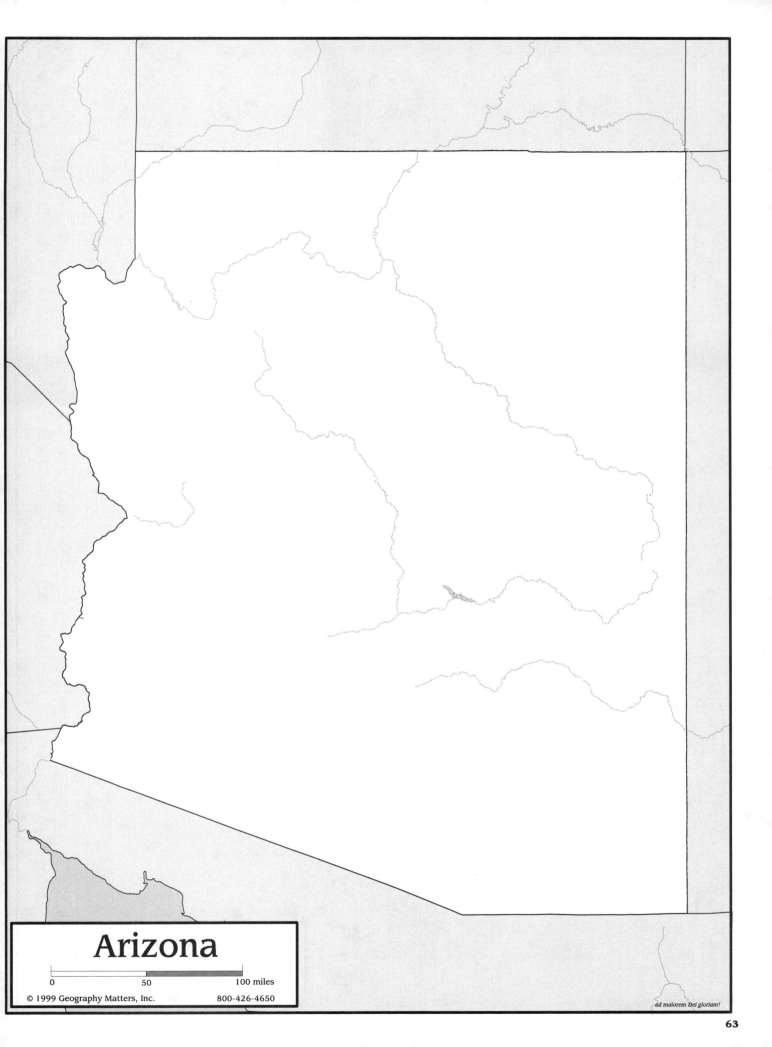

Arizona

0   50   100 miles

ad maiorem Dei gloriam!

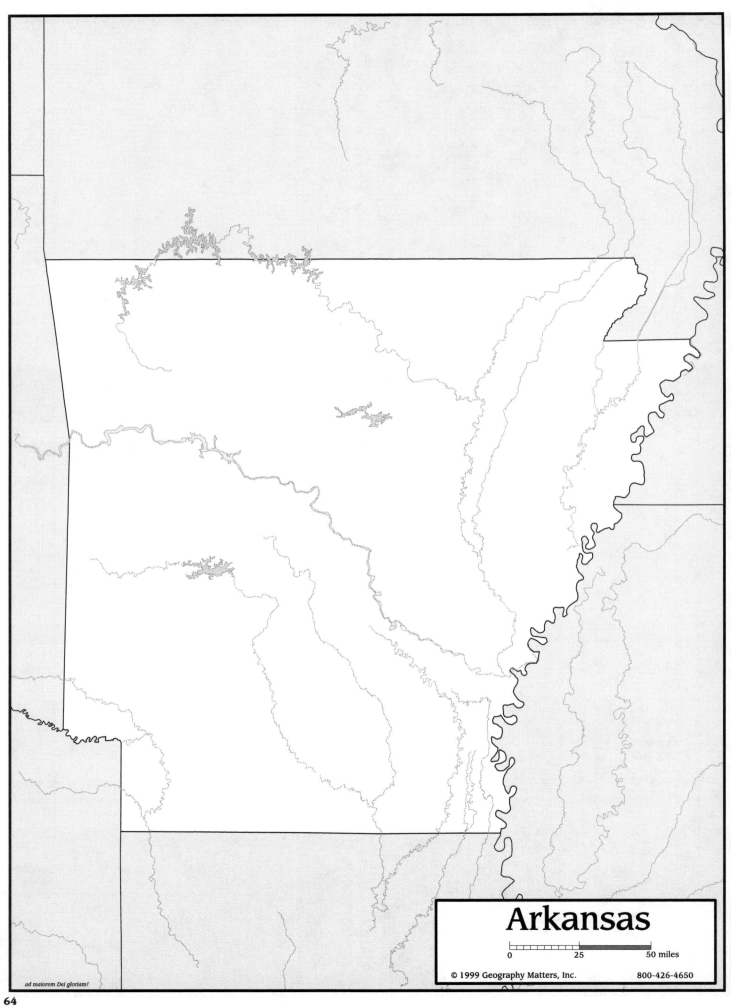

Arkansas

0   25   50 miles

ad maiorem Dei gloriam!

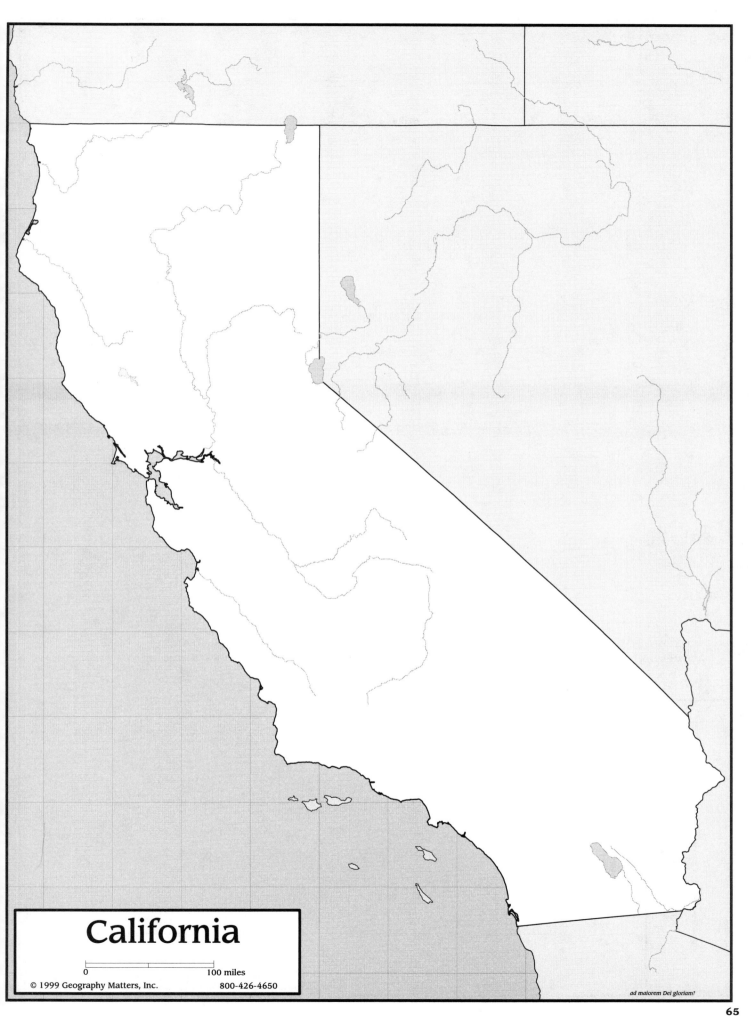

California

0   100 miles

© 1999 Geography Matters, Inc.   800-426-4650

ad maiorem Dei gloriam!

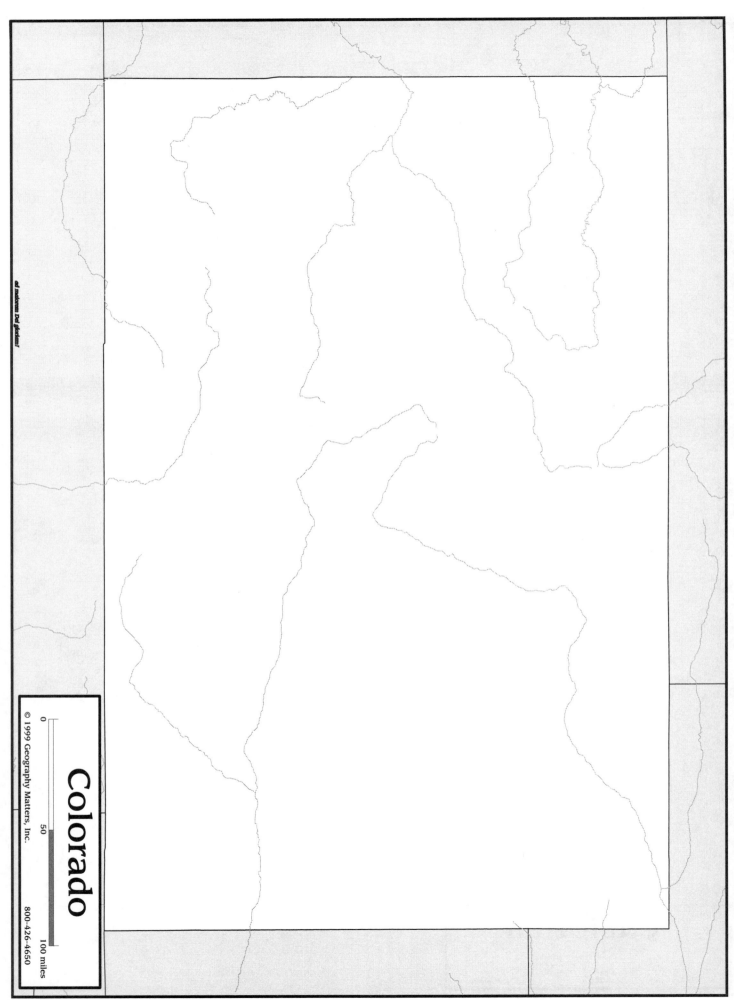

Colorado

© 1999 Geography Matters, Inc.   800-426-4650

ad maiorem Dei gloriam!

0   50   100 miles

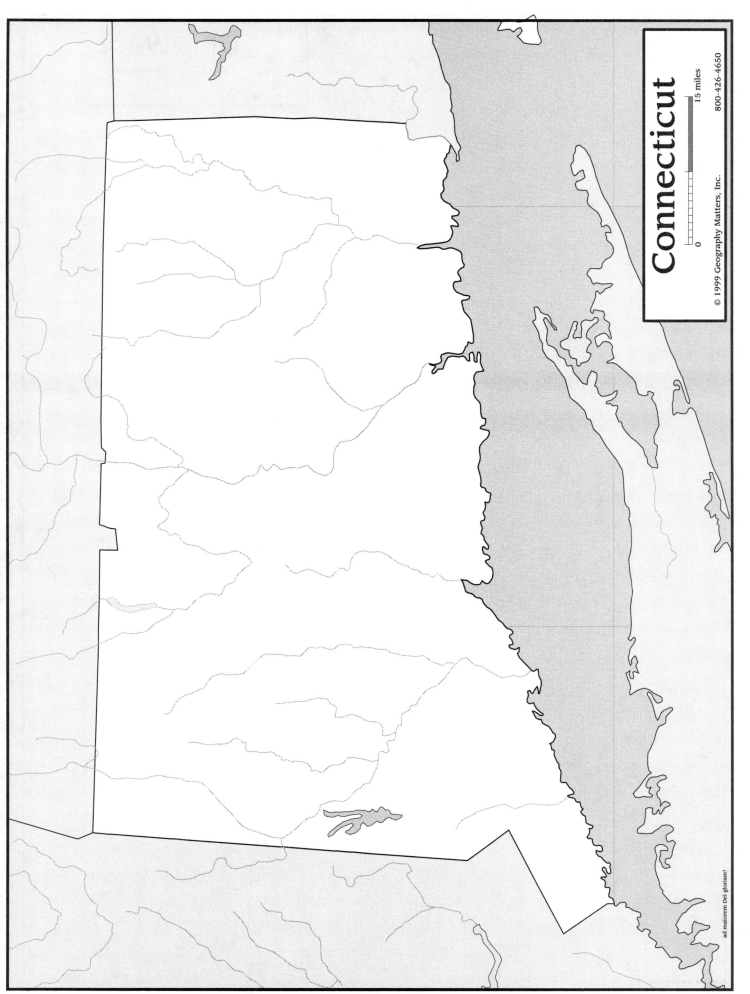

Connecticut

0 |━━━━━━━| 15 miles

800-426-4650

© 1999 Geography Matters, Inc.

ad maiorem Dei gloriam!

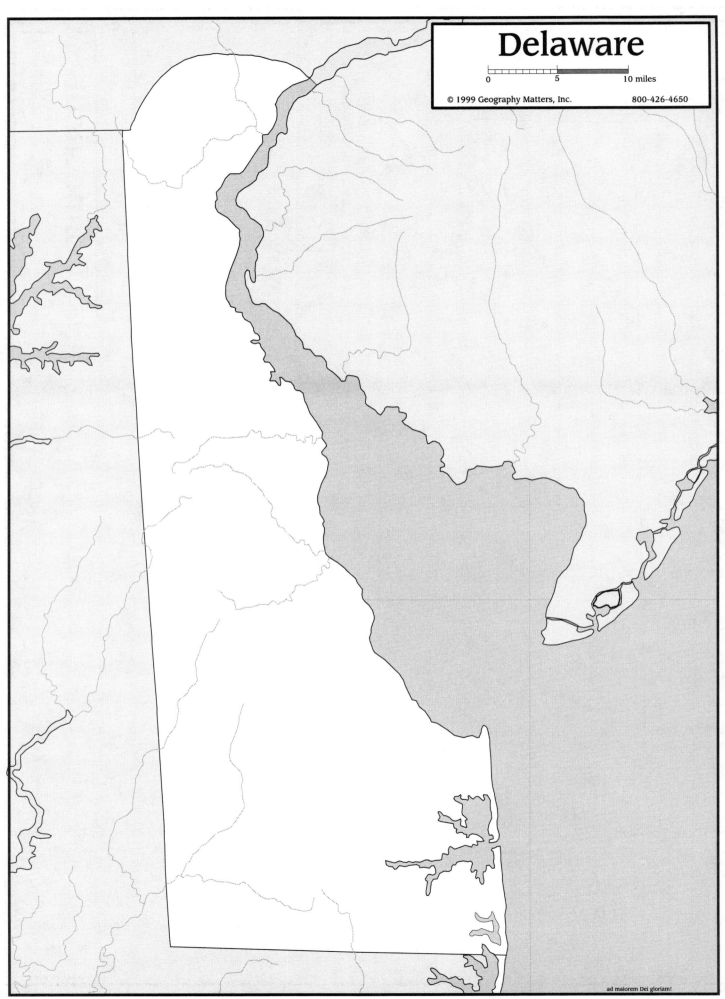

Delaware

0   5   10 miles

© 1999 Geography Matters, Inc.   800-426-4650

ad maiorem Dei gloriam!

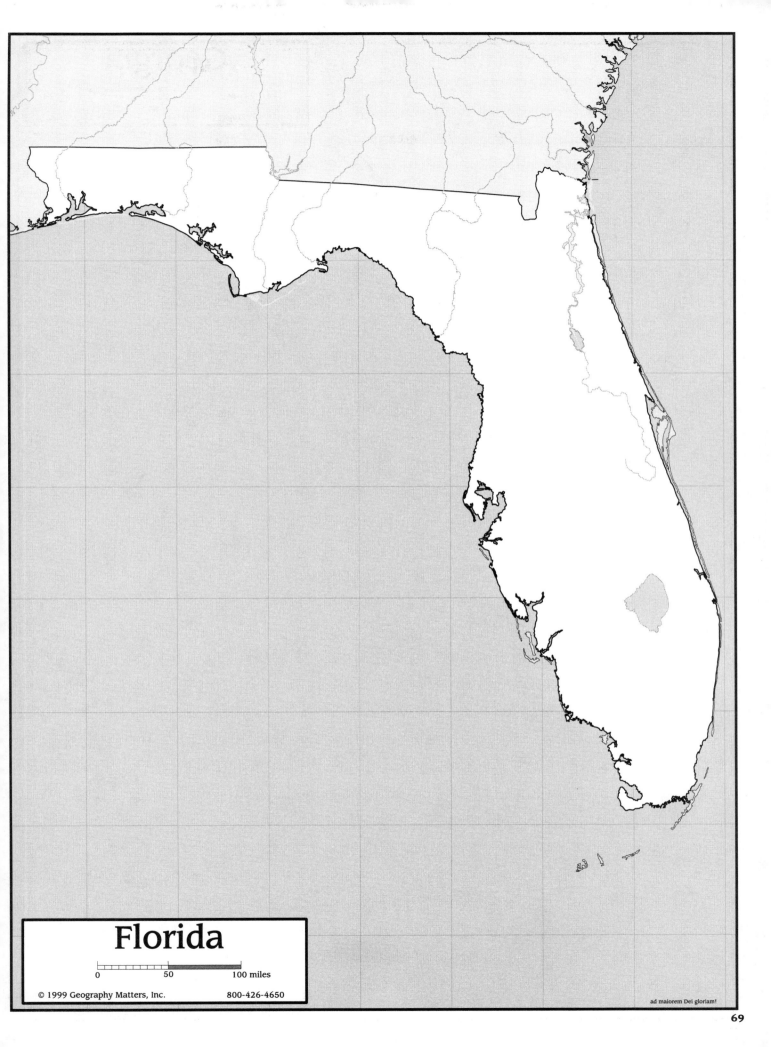

Florida

0   50   100 miles

© 1999 Geography Matters, Inc.   800-426-4650

ad maiorem Dei gloriam!

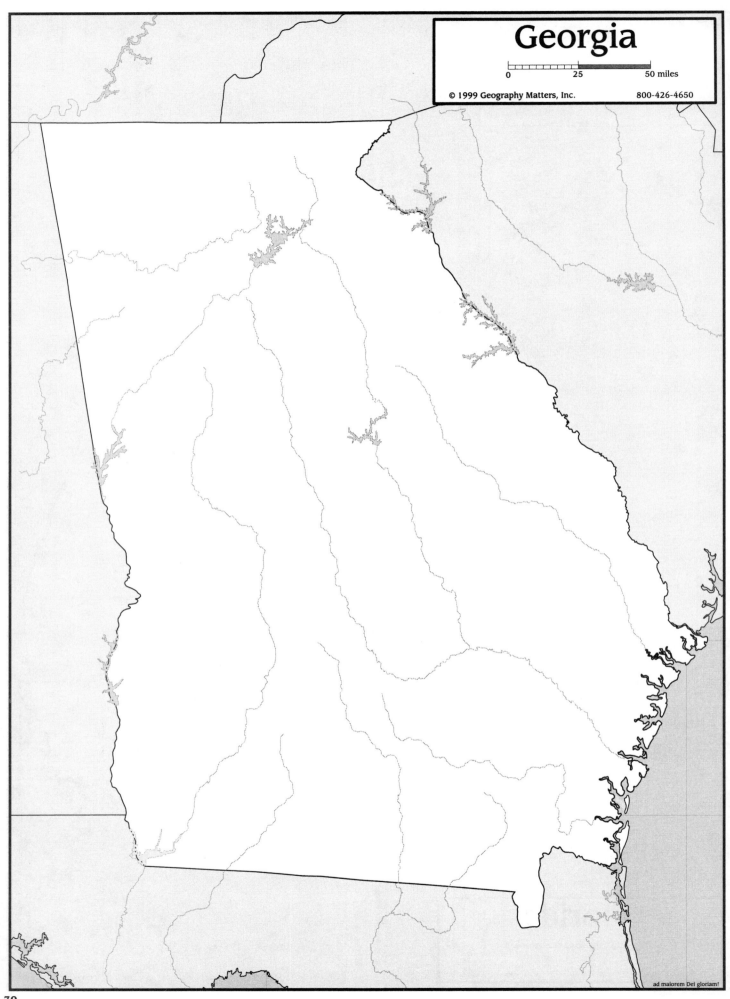

Georgia

0   25   50 miles

© 1999 Geography Matters, Inc.   800-426-4650

ad maiorem Dei gloriam!

70

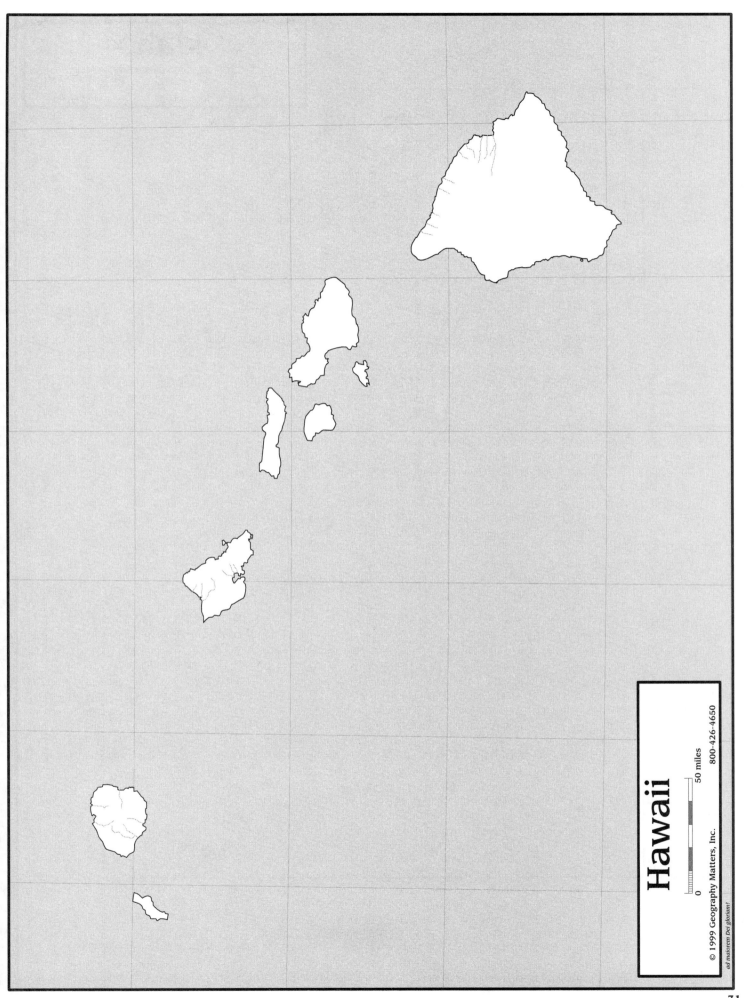

Hawaii

0   50 miles

800-426-4650

ad maiorem Dei gloriam!

71

Idaho

0 50 100 miles

© 1999 Geography Matters, Inc.   800-426-4650

ad maiorem Dei gloriam!

72

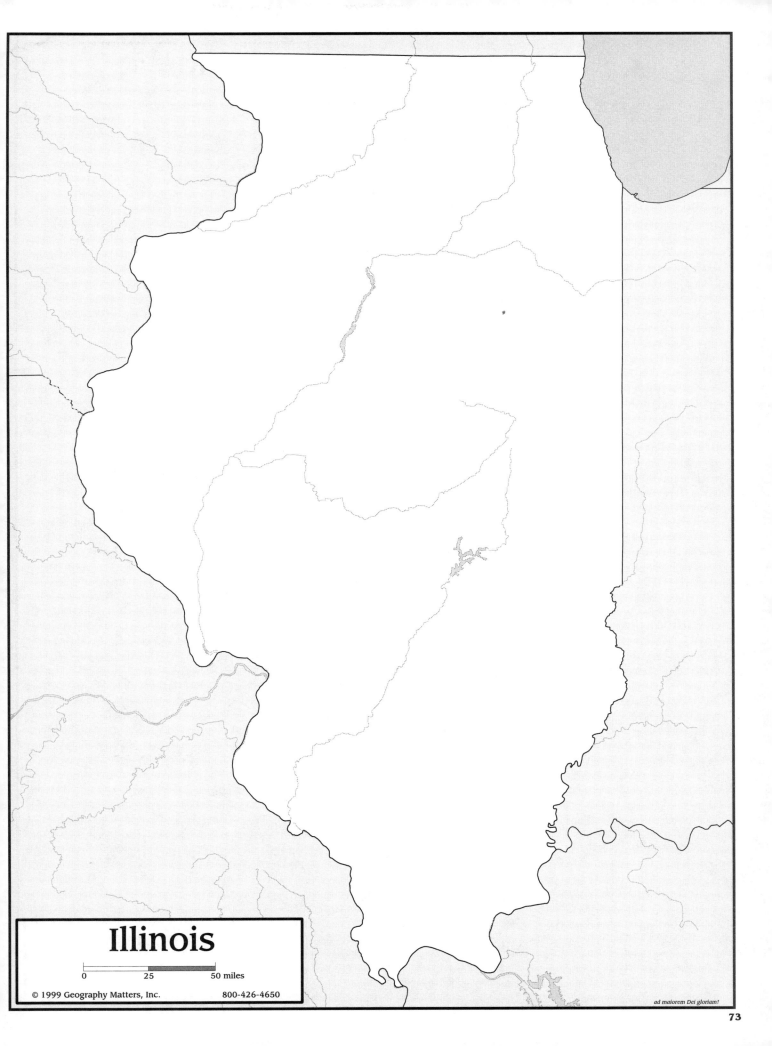

Illinois

0   25   50 miles

© 1999 Geography Matters, Inc.   800-426-4650

ad maiorem Dei gloriam!

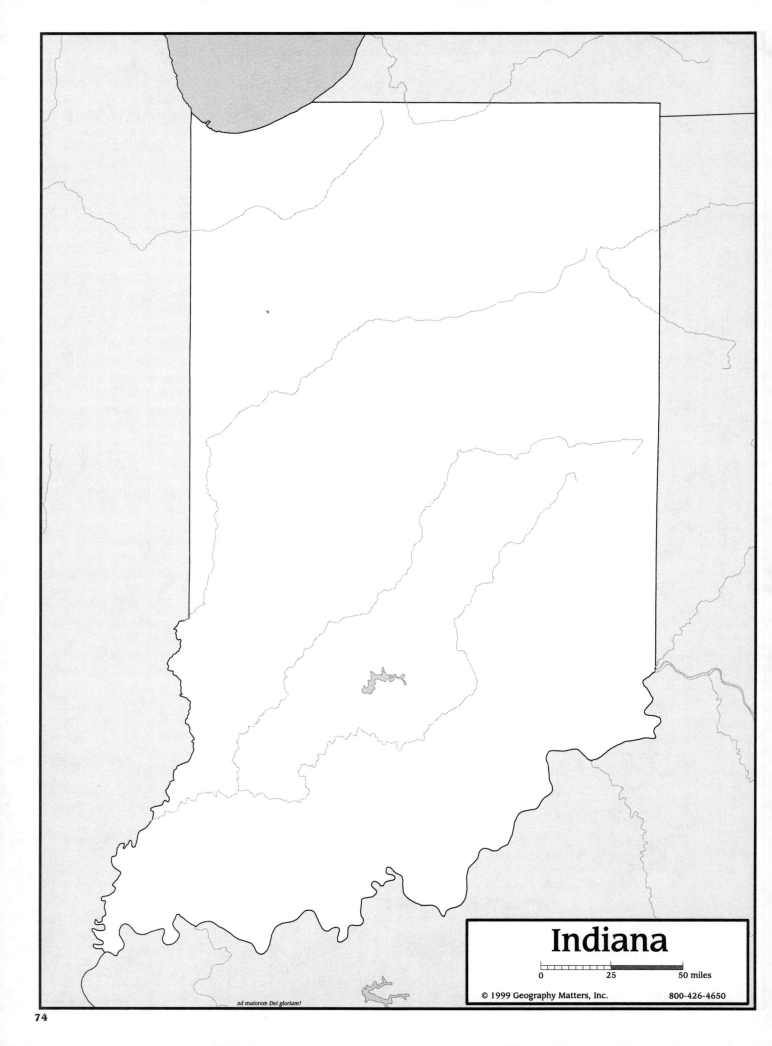

Indiana

0   25   50 miles

© 1999 Geography Matters, Inc.   800-426-4650

ad maiorem Dei gloriam!

74

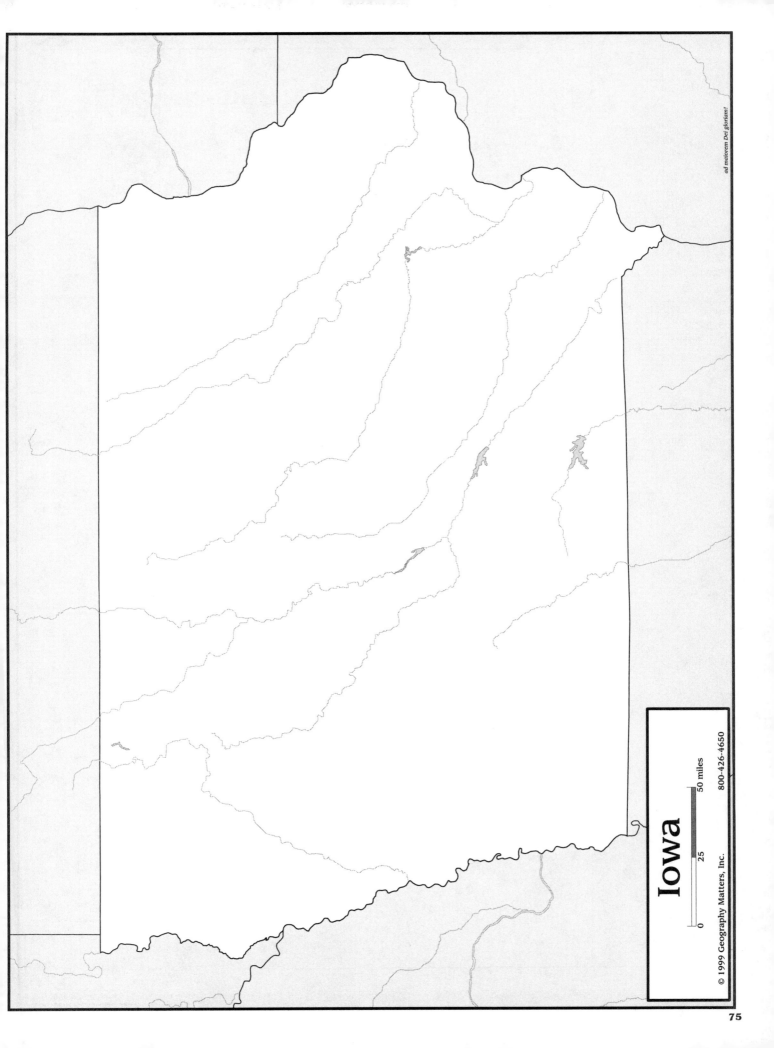

Iowa

0   25   50 miles

800-426-4650

© 1999 Geography Matters, Inc.

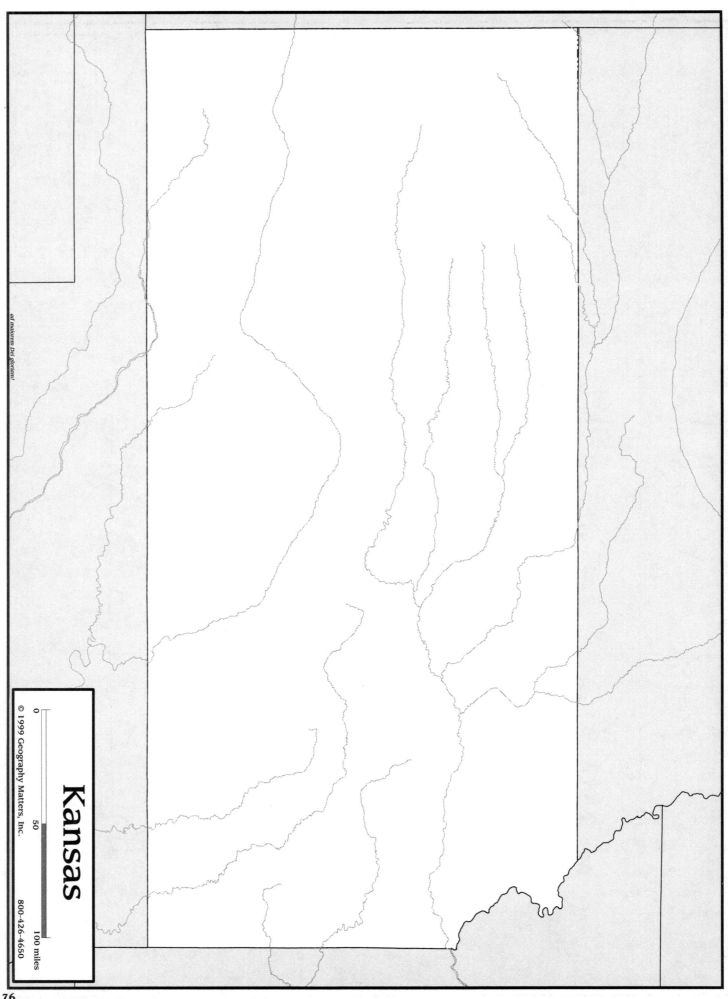

Kansas

0 50 100 miles

© 1999 Geography Matters, Inc.   800-426-4650

ad maiorem Dei gloriam!

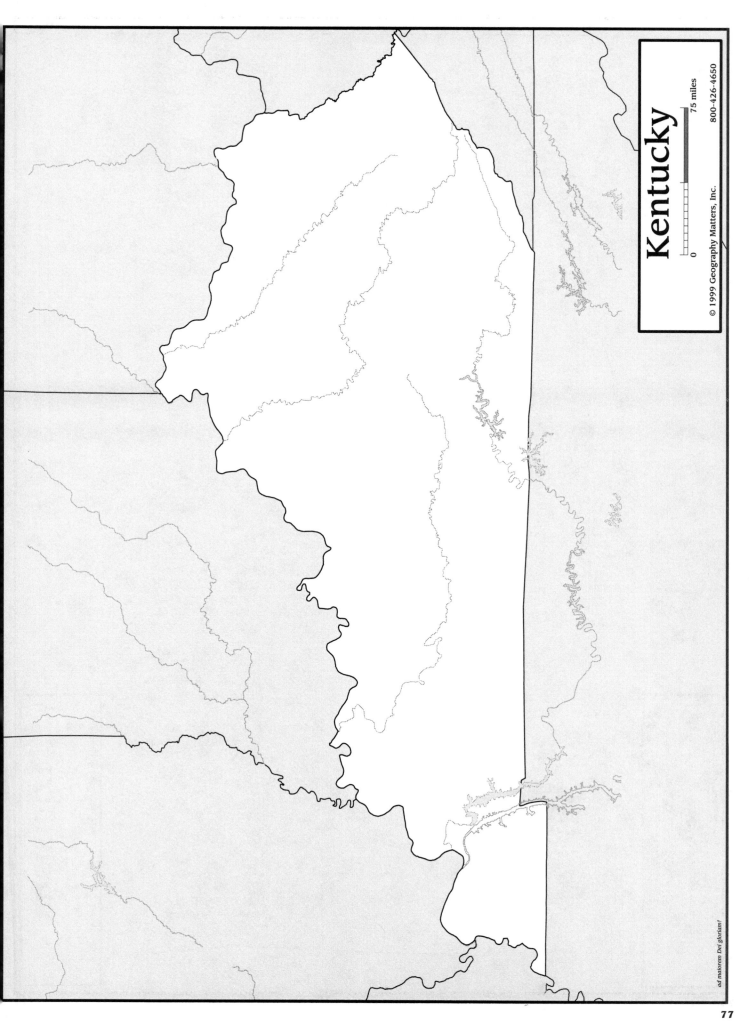

Kentucky

0 |||||||| 75 miles

© 1999 Geography Matters, Inc.

800-426-4650

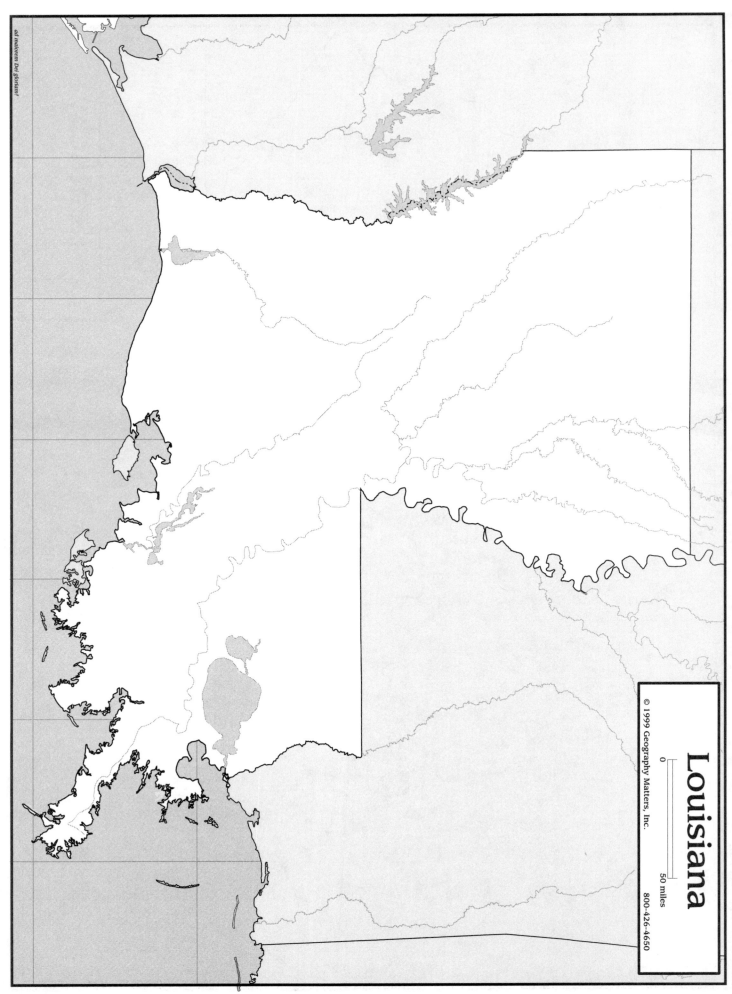

Louisiana

© 1999 Geography Matters, Inc.

0   50 miles

800-426-4650

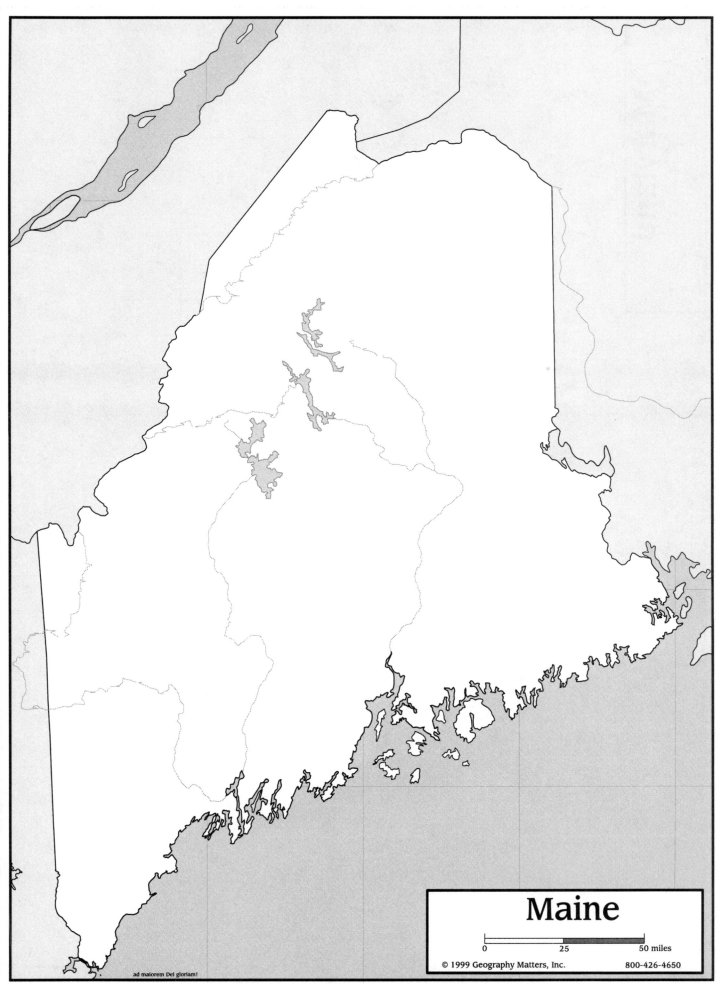

Maine

0   25   50 miles

© 1999 Geography Matters, Inc.   800-426-4650

ad maiorem Dei gloriam!

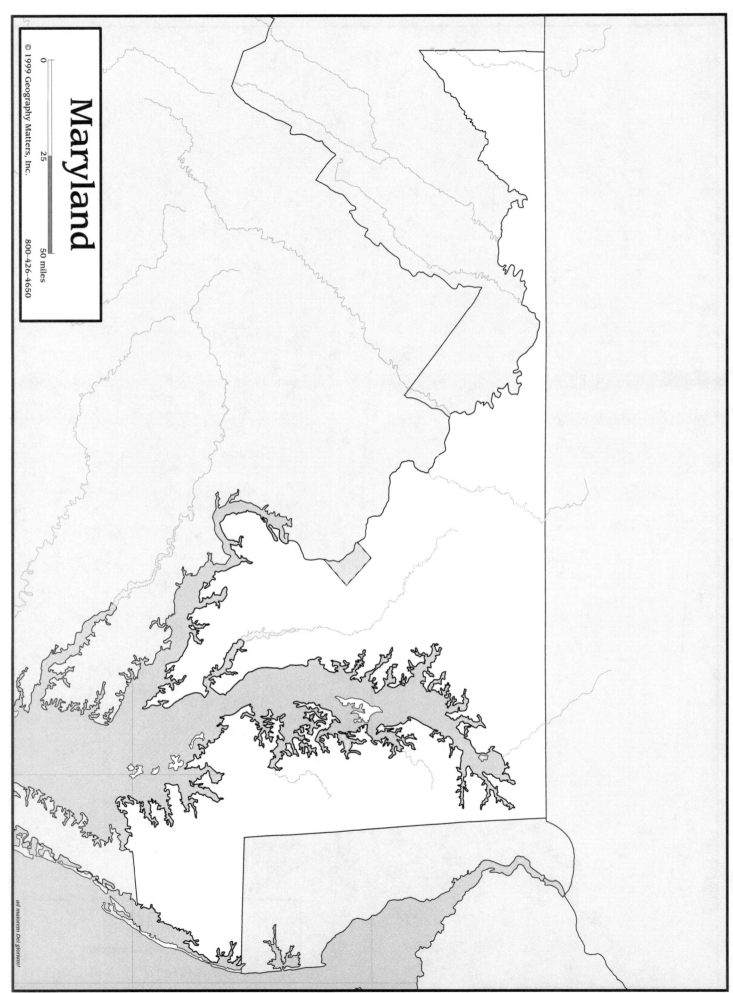

Maryland

© 1999 Geography Matters, Inc.   800-426-4650

0   25   50 miles

ad maiorem Dei gloriam!

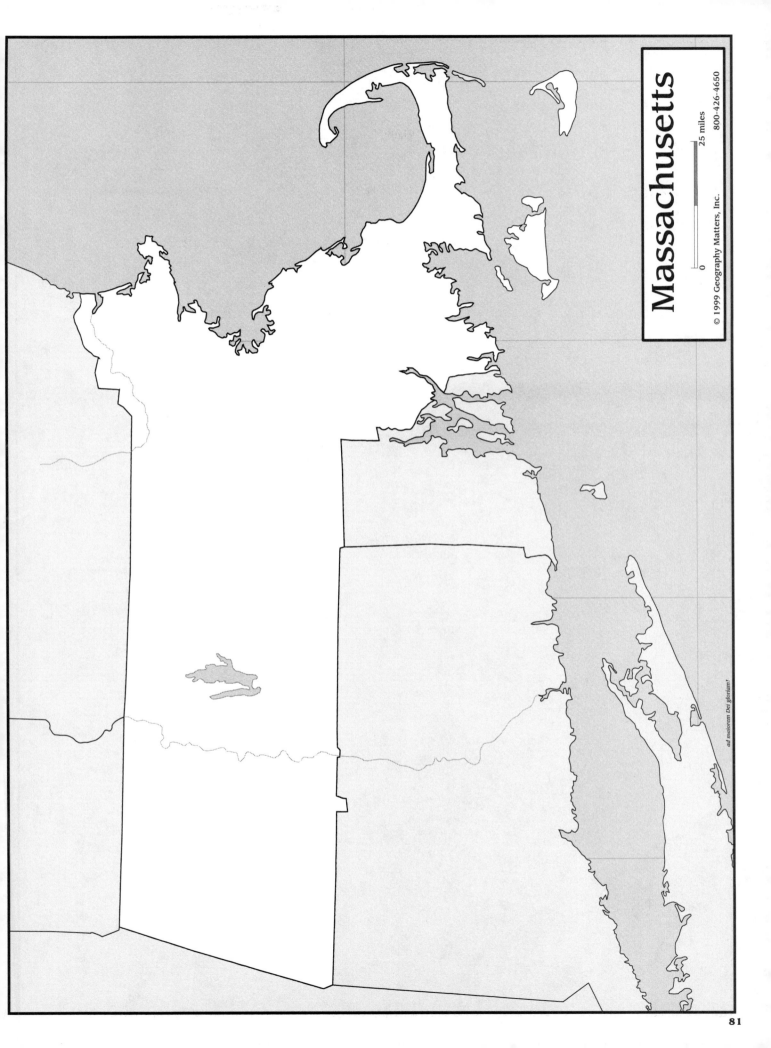

Massachusetts

25 miles

0

© 1999 Geography Matters, Inc.

800-426-4650

ad maiorem Dei gloriam!

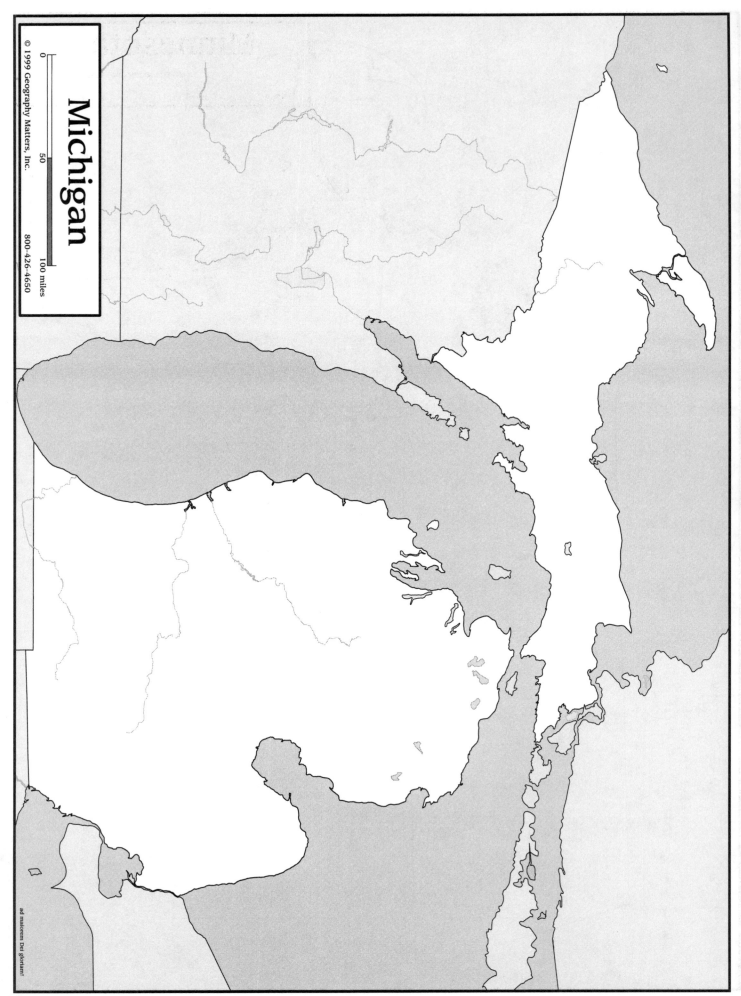

Michigan

© 1999 Geography Matters, Inc.   800-426-4650

0   50   100 miles

ad maiorem Dei gloriam!

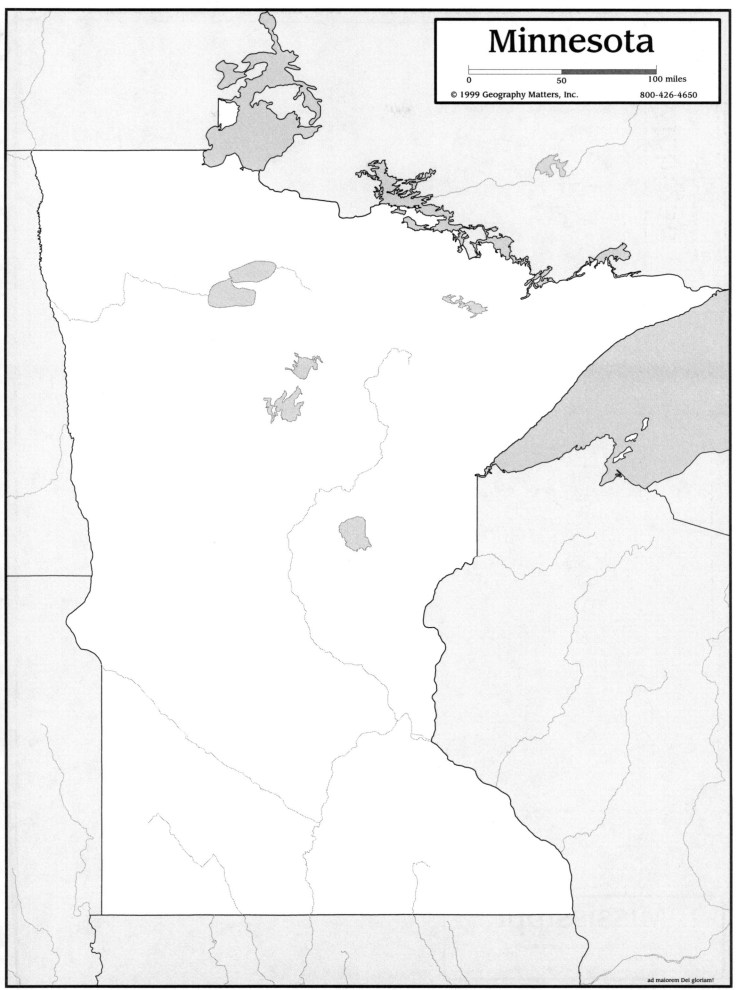

Minnesota

0   50   100 miles

© 1999 Geography Matters, Inc.   800-426-4650

ad maiorem Dei gloriam!

83

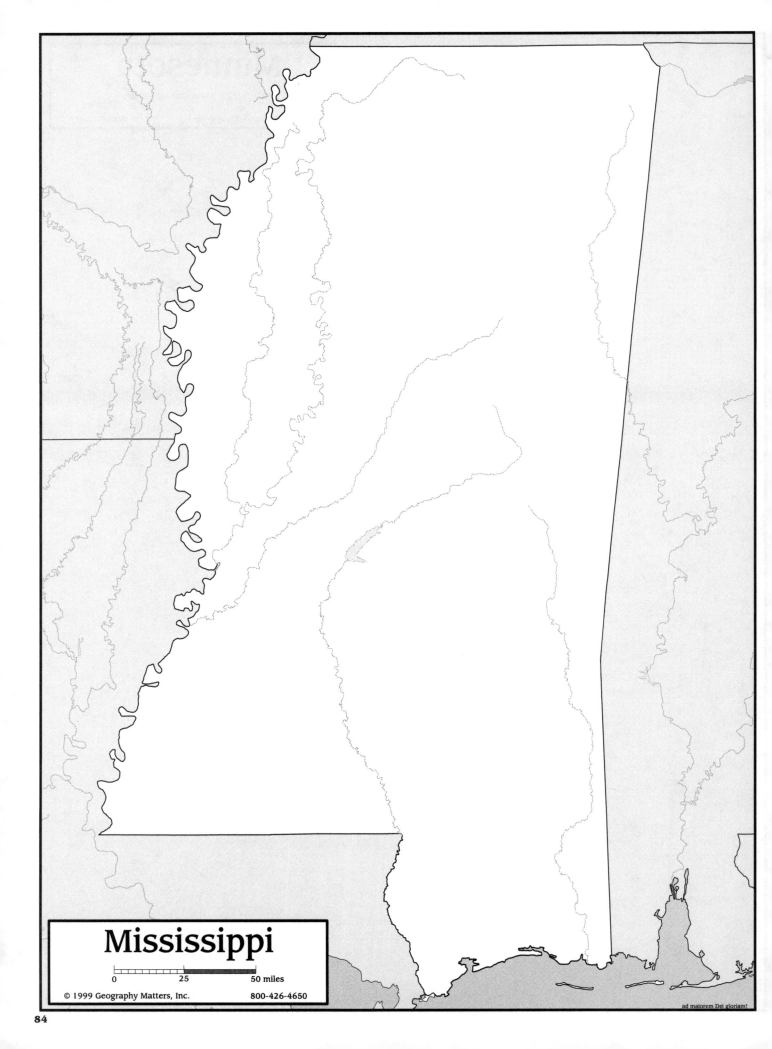

Mississippi

0   25   50 miles

© 1999 Geography Matters, Inc.   800-426-4650

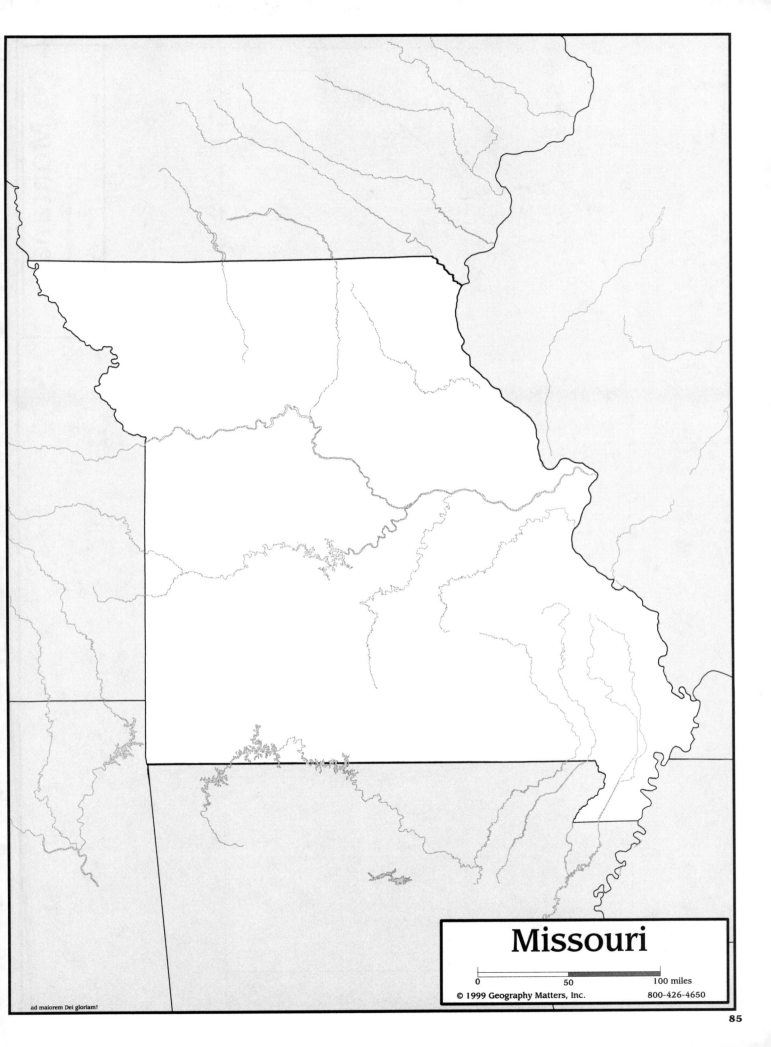

Missouri

0   50   100 miles

© 1999 Geography Matters, Inc.   800-426-4650

ad maiorem Dei gloriam!

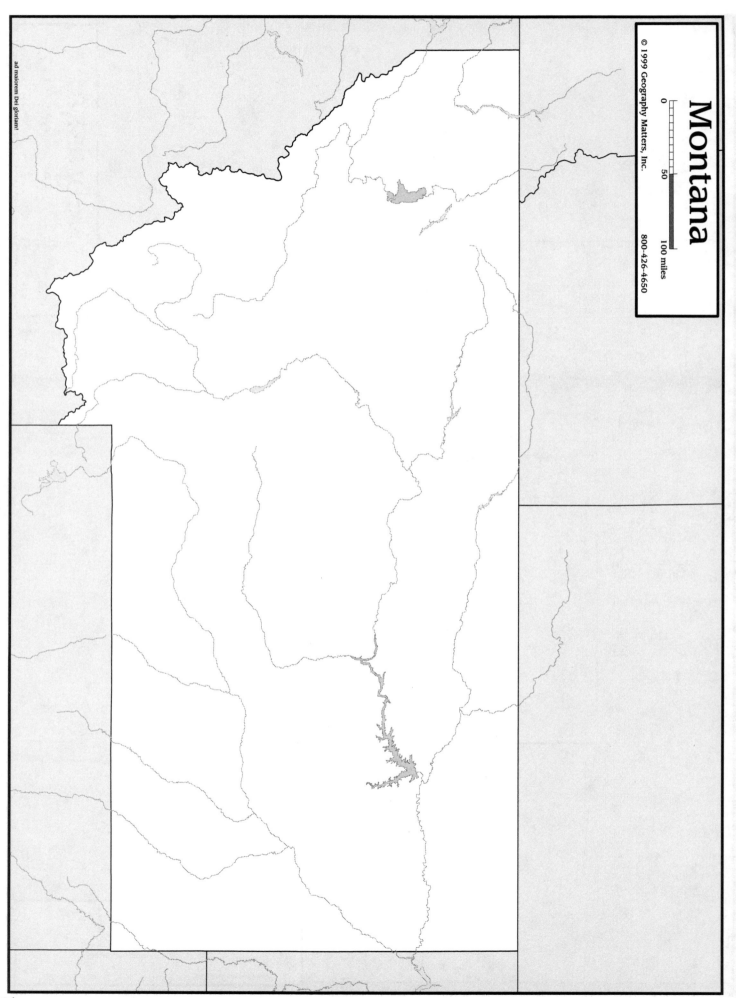

© 1999 Geography Matters, Inc.

800-426-4650

0   50   100 miles

ad maiorem Dei gloriam!

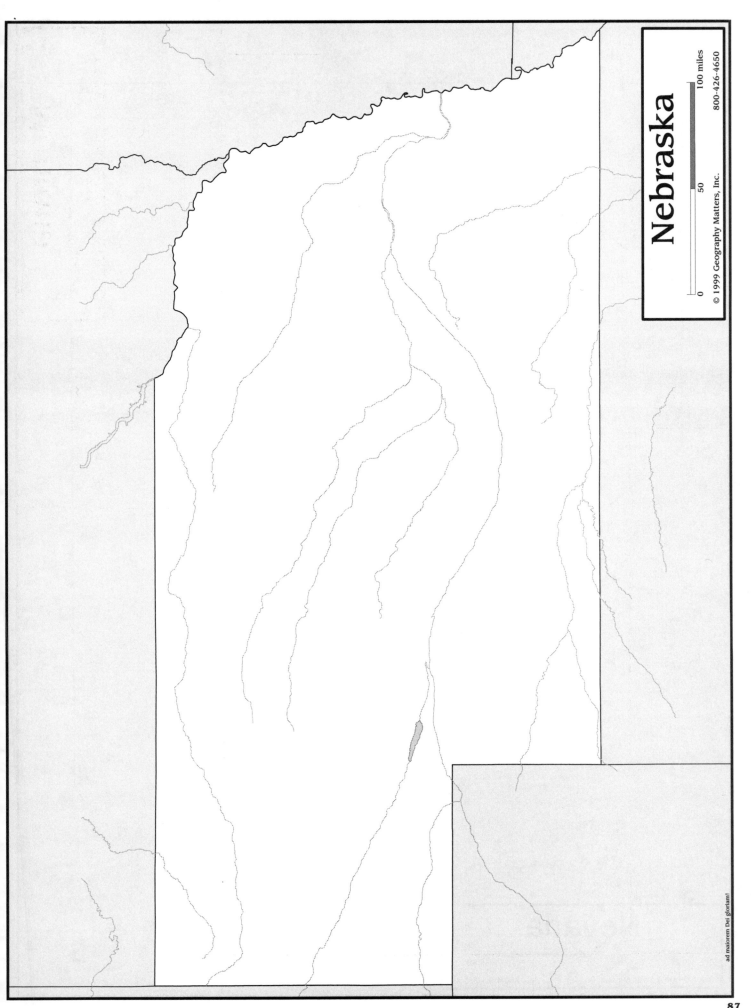

Nebraska

0   50   100 miles

ad maiorem Dei gloriam!

Nevada

0   50   100 miles

© 1999 Geography Matters, Inc.   800-426-4650

ad maiorem Dei gloriam!

New Hampshire

0　　25　　50 miles

© 1999 Geography Matters, Inc.　　　800-426-4650

ad maiorem Dei gloriam!

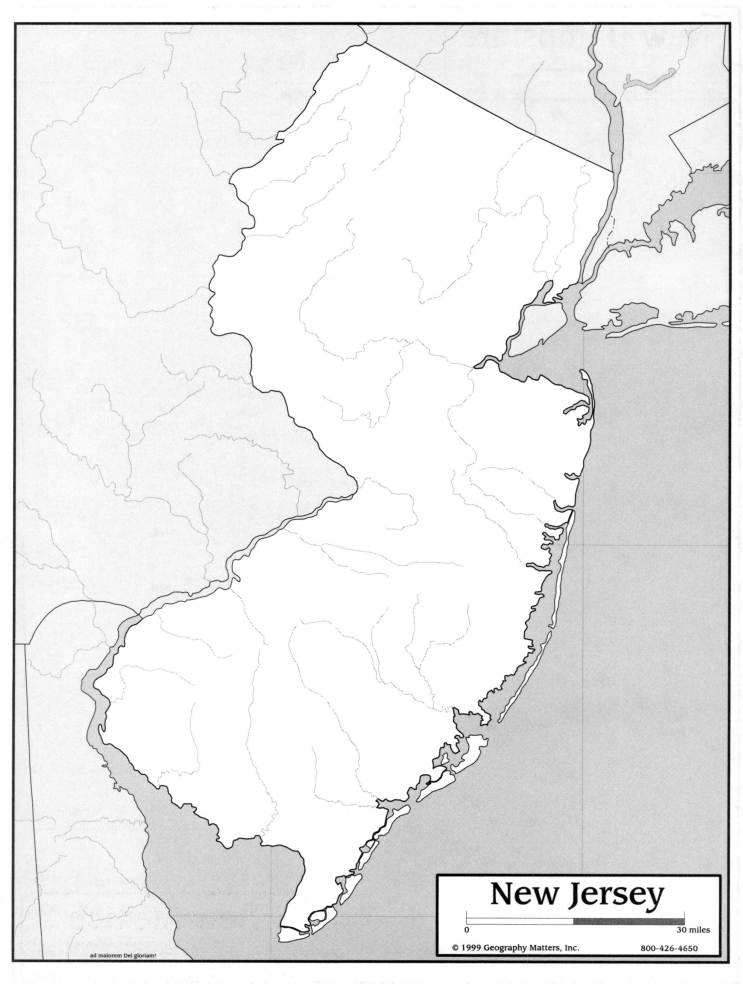

New Jersey

0   30 miles

© 1999 Geography Matters, Inc.   800-426-4650

ad maiorem Dei gloriam!

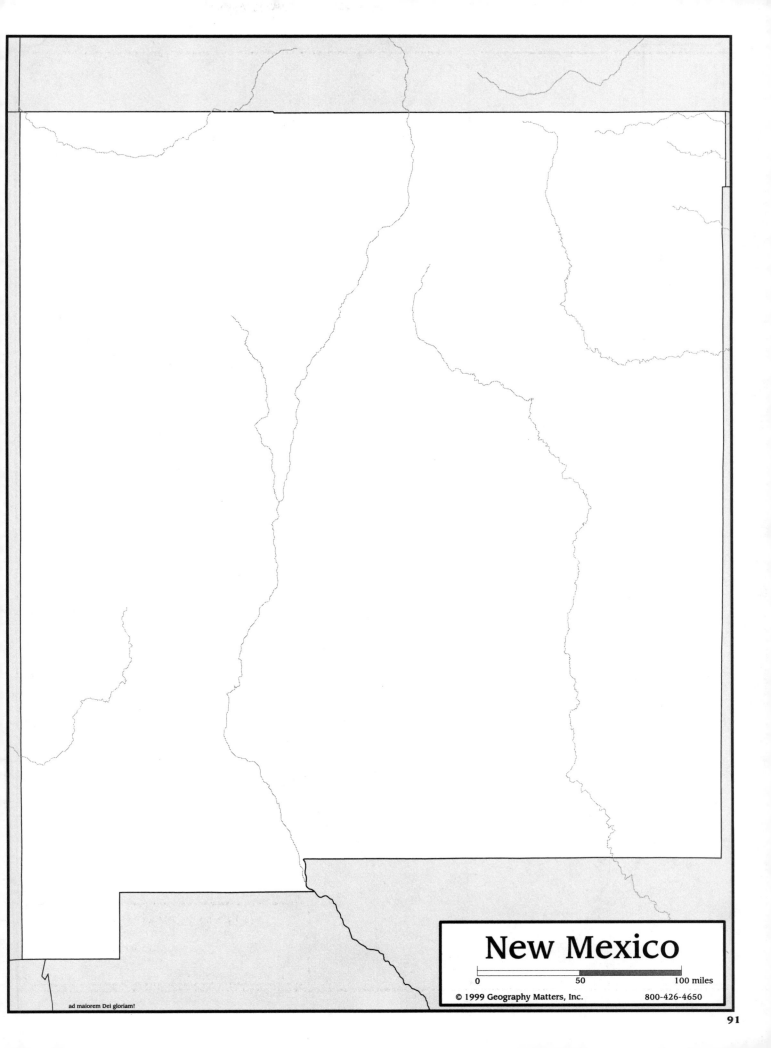

New Mexico

0   50   100 miles

© 1999 Geography Matters, Inc.   800-426-4650

ad maiorem Dei gloriam!

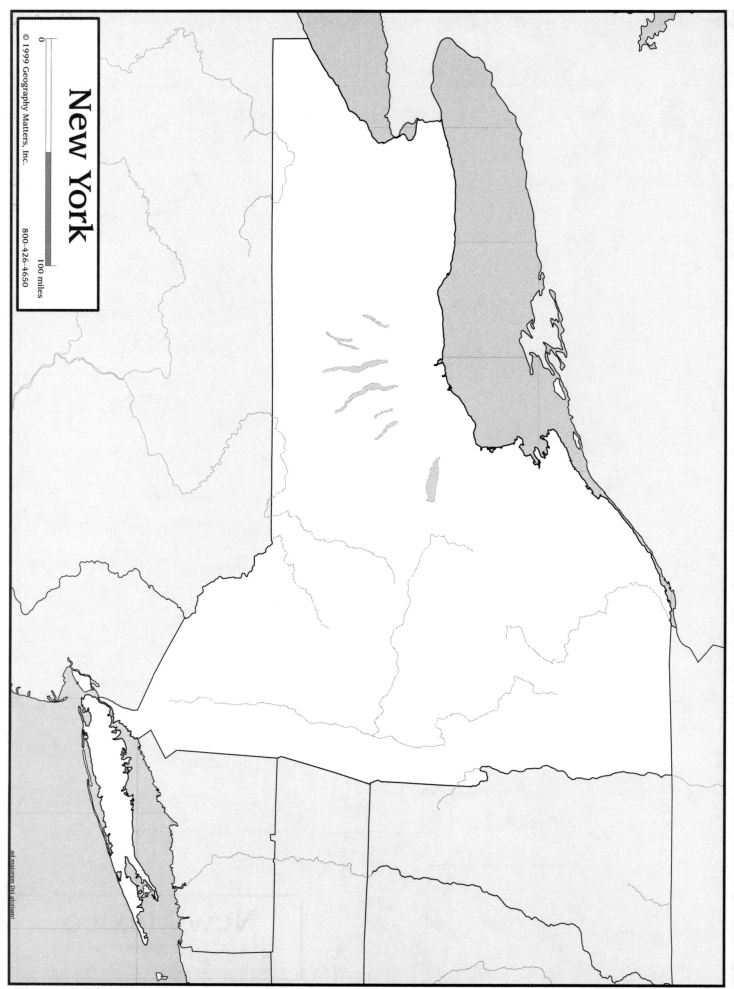

New York

© 1999 Geography Matters, Inc.

800-426-4650

0

100 miles

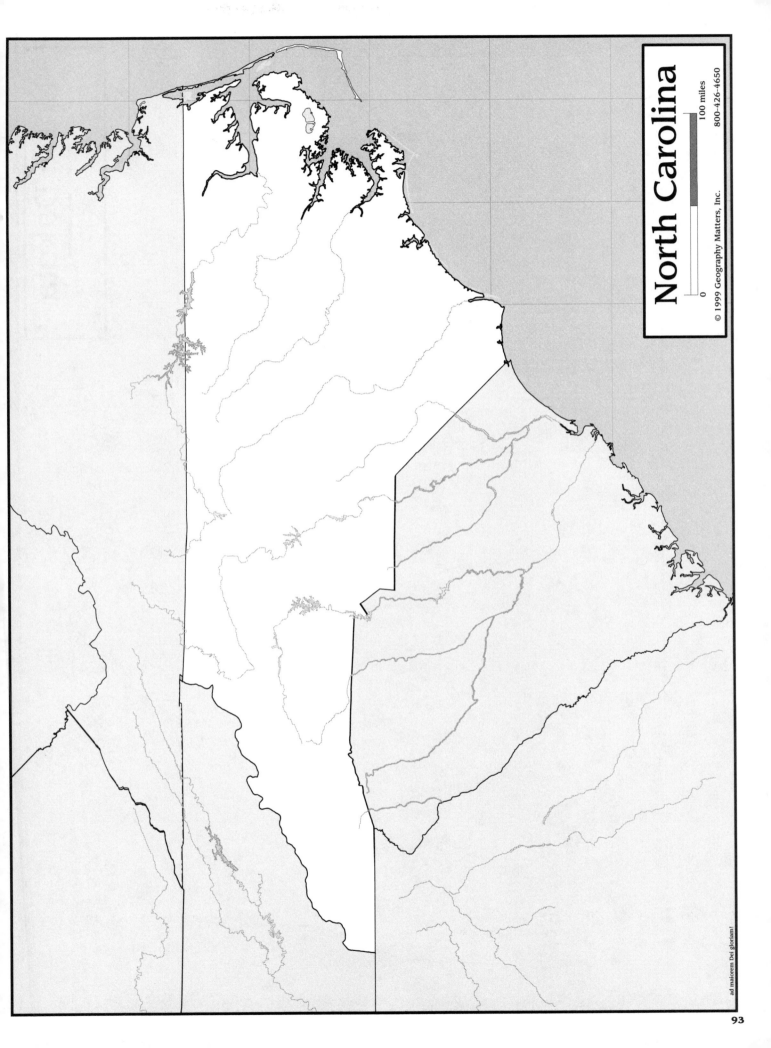

North Carolina

0 100 miles

© 1999 Geography Matters, Inc.

800-426-4650

ad maiorem Dei gloriam!

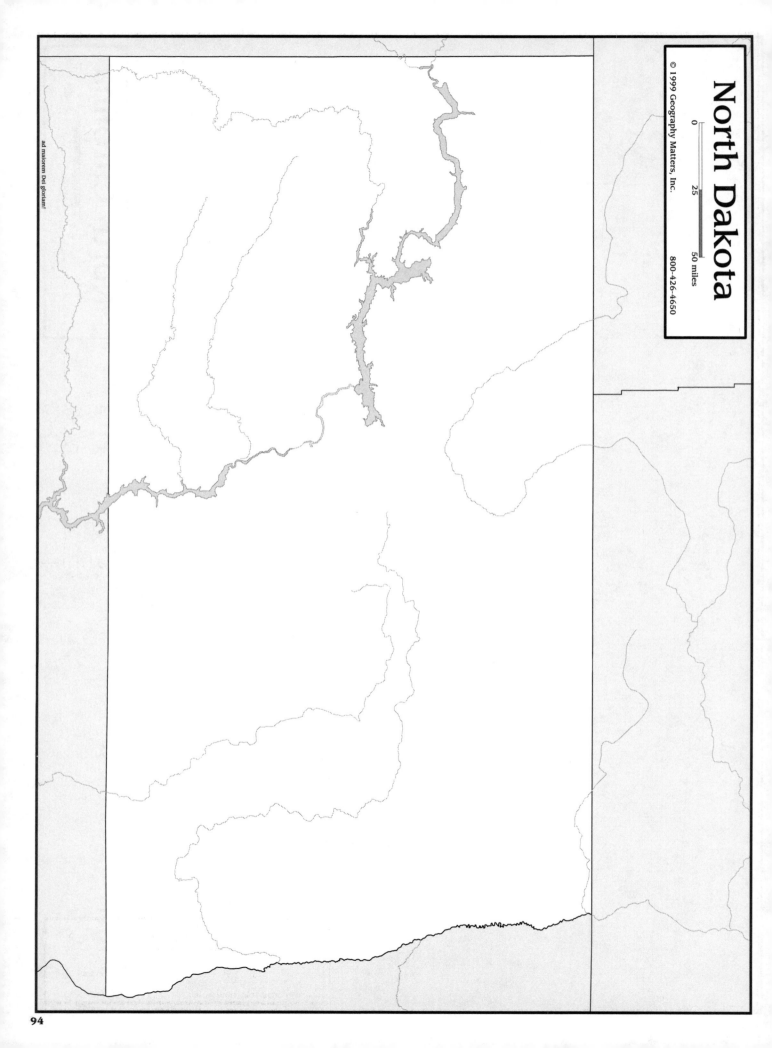

North Dakota

0   25   50 miles

ad maiorem Dei gloriam!

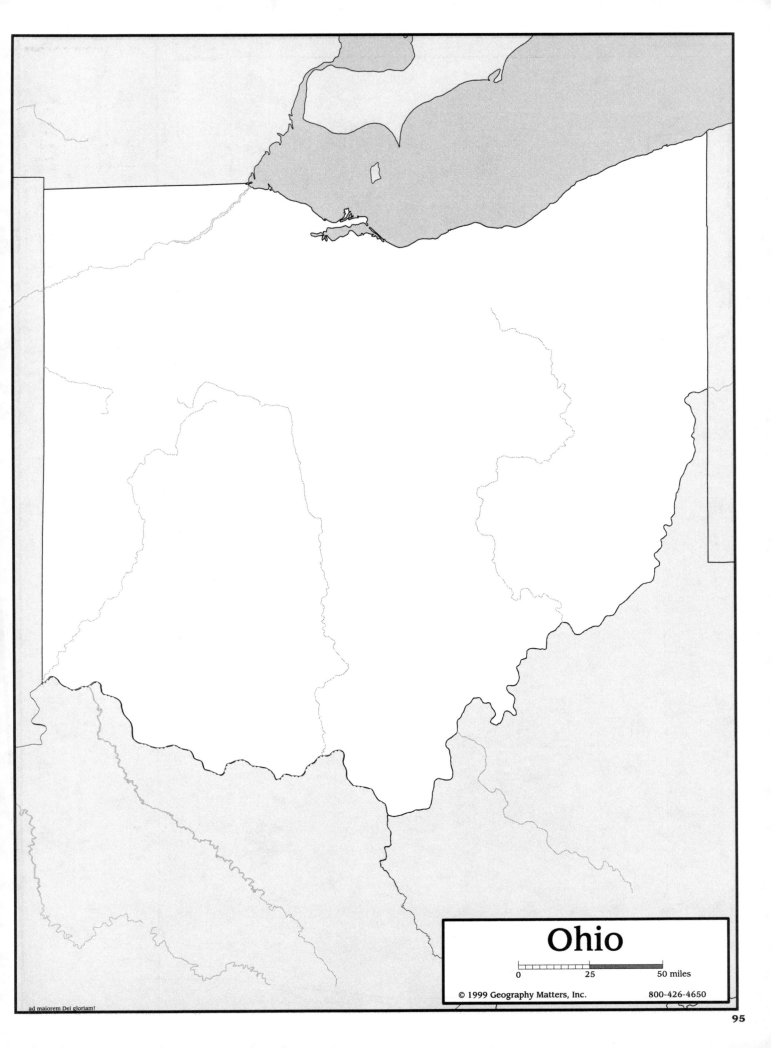

Ohio

0　　　25　　　50 miles

© 1999 Geography Matters, Inc.　　　800-426-4650

ad maiorem Dei gloriam!

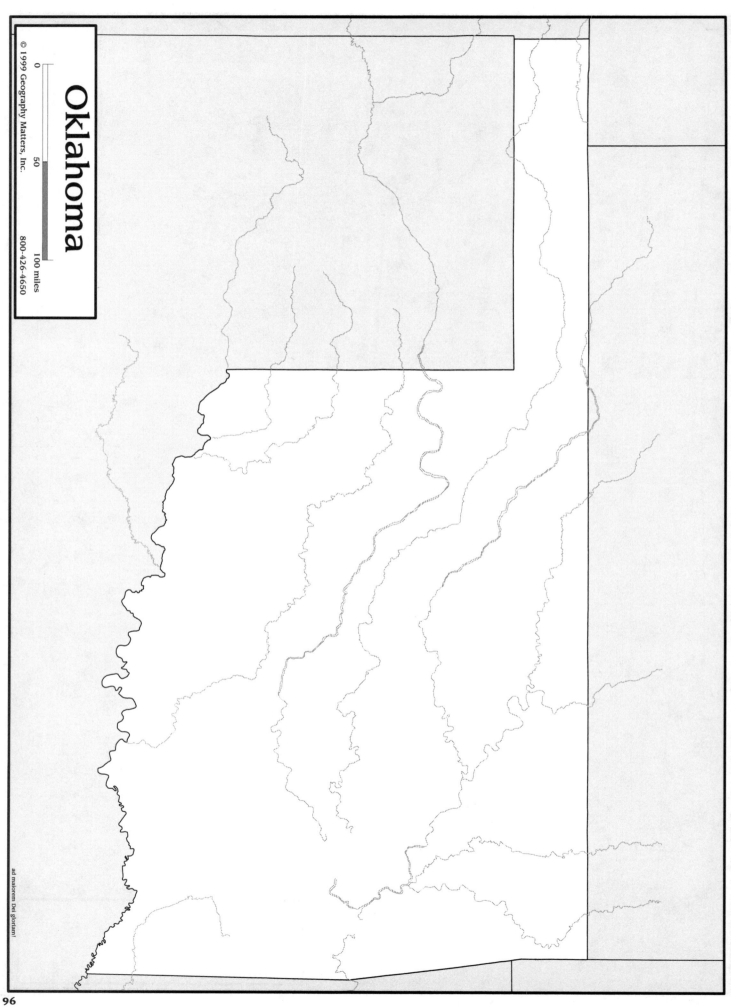

Oklahoma

© 1999 Geography Matters, Inc.

800-426-4650

0
50
100 miles

ad maiorem Dei gloriam!

96

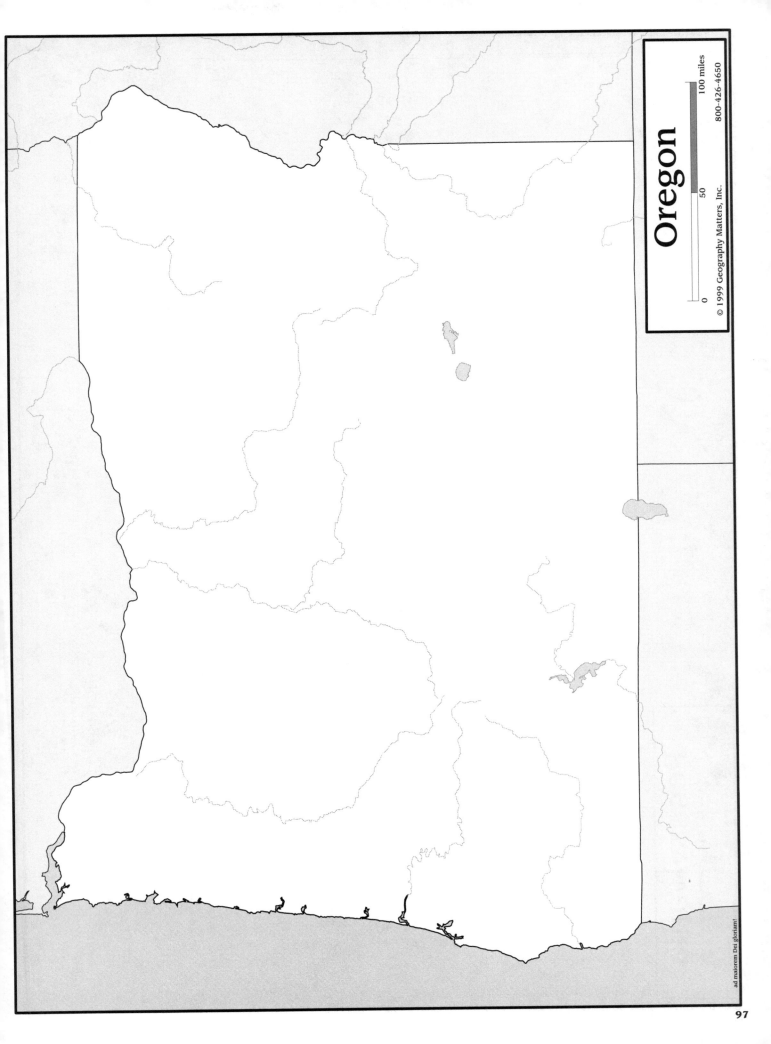

Oregon

© 1999 Geography Matters, Inc.

800-426-4650

0   50   100 miles

ad maiorem Dei gloriam!

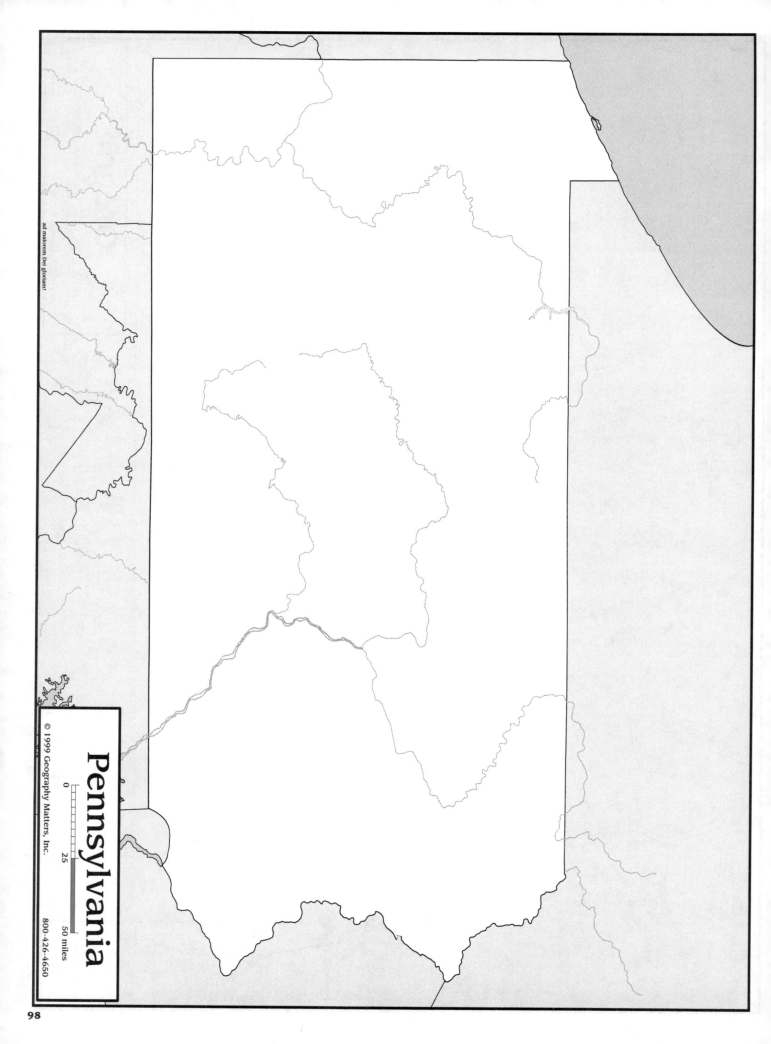

Pennsylvania

0   25   50 miles

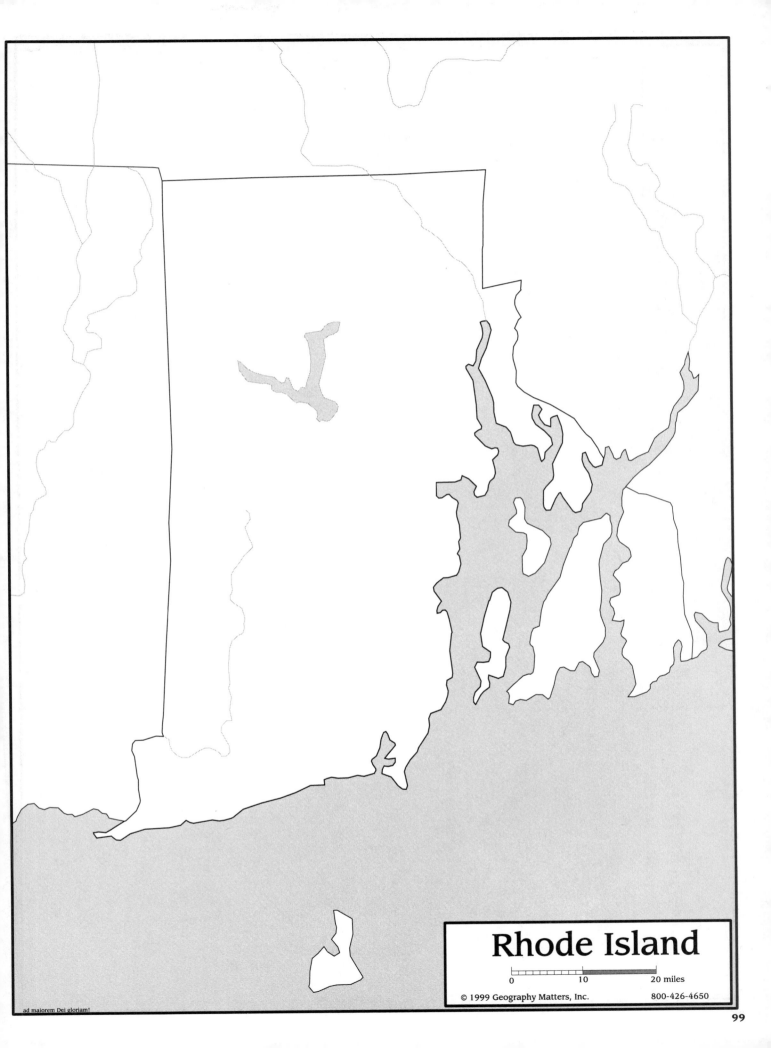

Rhode Island

0   10   20 miles

© 1999 Geography Matters, Inc.   800-426-4650

ad maiorem Dei gloriam!

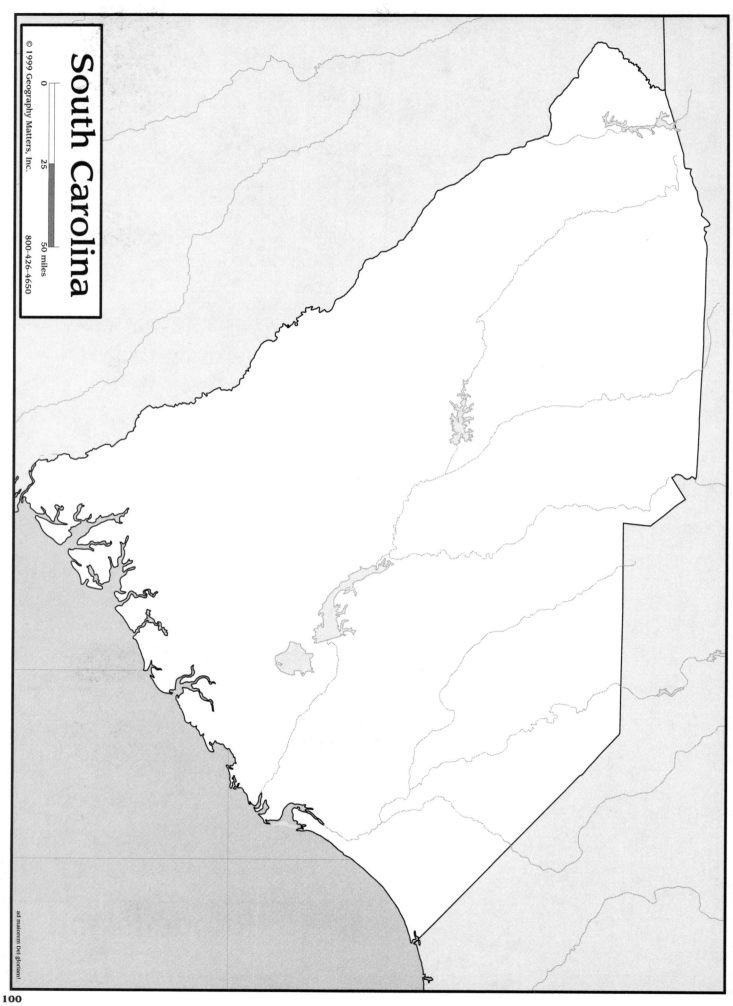

South Carolina

© 1999 Geography Matters, Inc.

0   25   50 miles

800-426-4650

ad maiorem Dei gloriam!

South Dakota

0   25   50 miles

800-426-4650

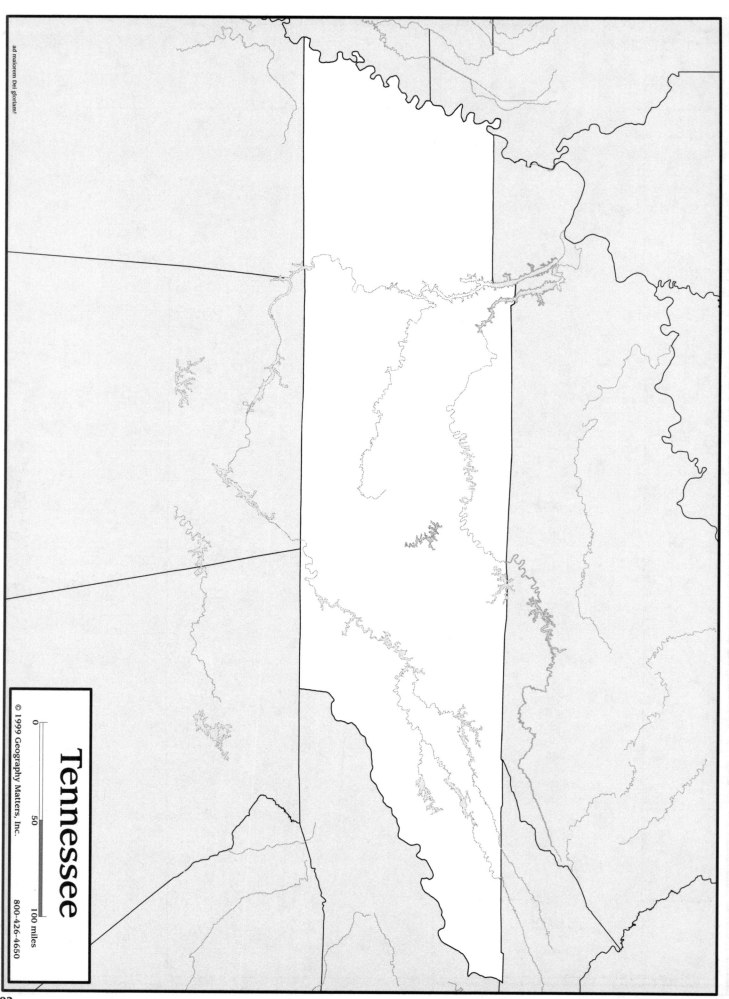

Tennessee

© 1999 Geography Matters, Inc.

0   50   100 miles

800-426-4650

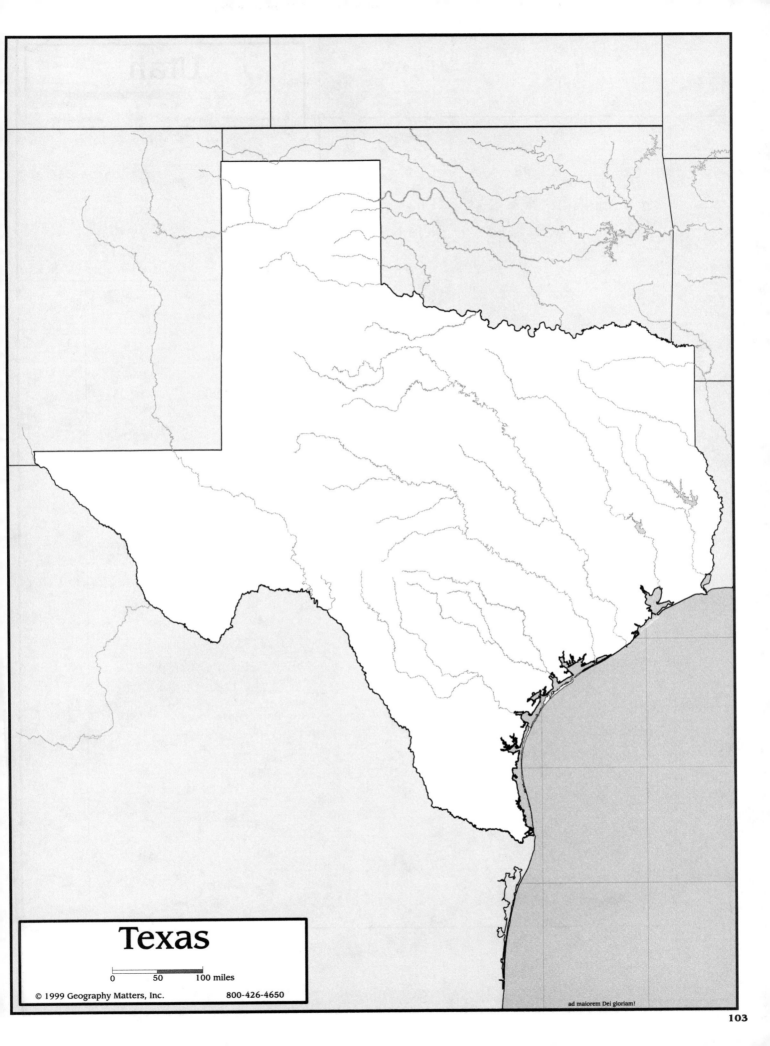

Texas

0   50   100 miles

© 1999 Geography Matters, Inc.   800-426-4650

ad maiorem Dei gloriam!

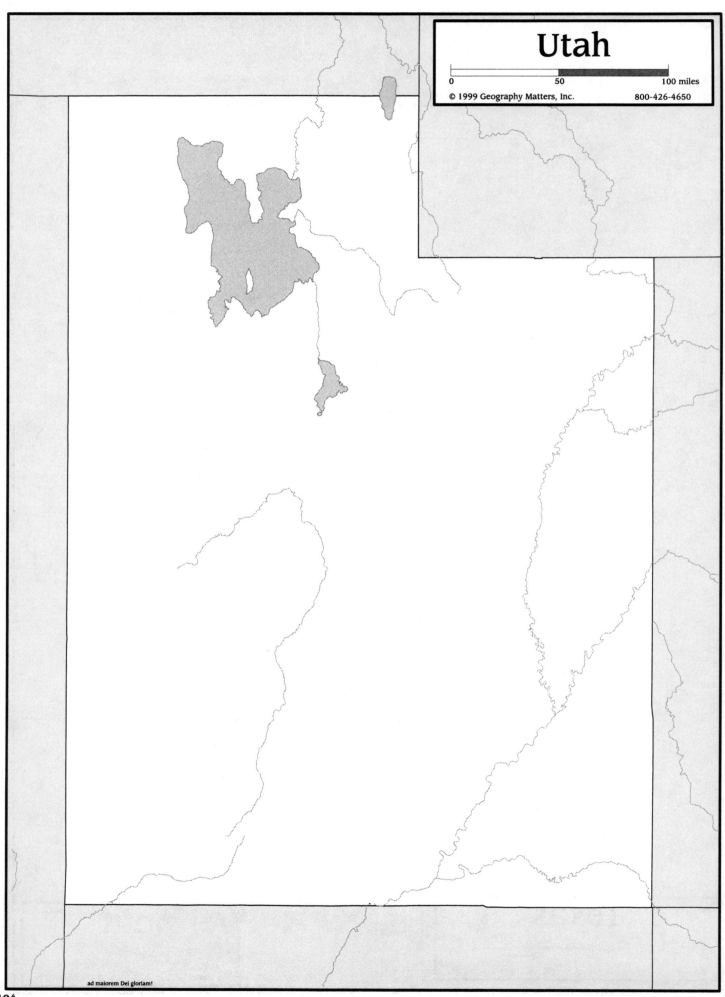

Utah

0   50   100 miles

© 1999 Geography Matters, Inc.   800-426-4650

ad maiorem Dei gloriam!

Vermont

0　25　50 miles

© 1999 Geography Matters, Inc.　　　800-426-4650

ad maiorem Dei gloriam!

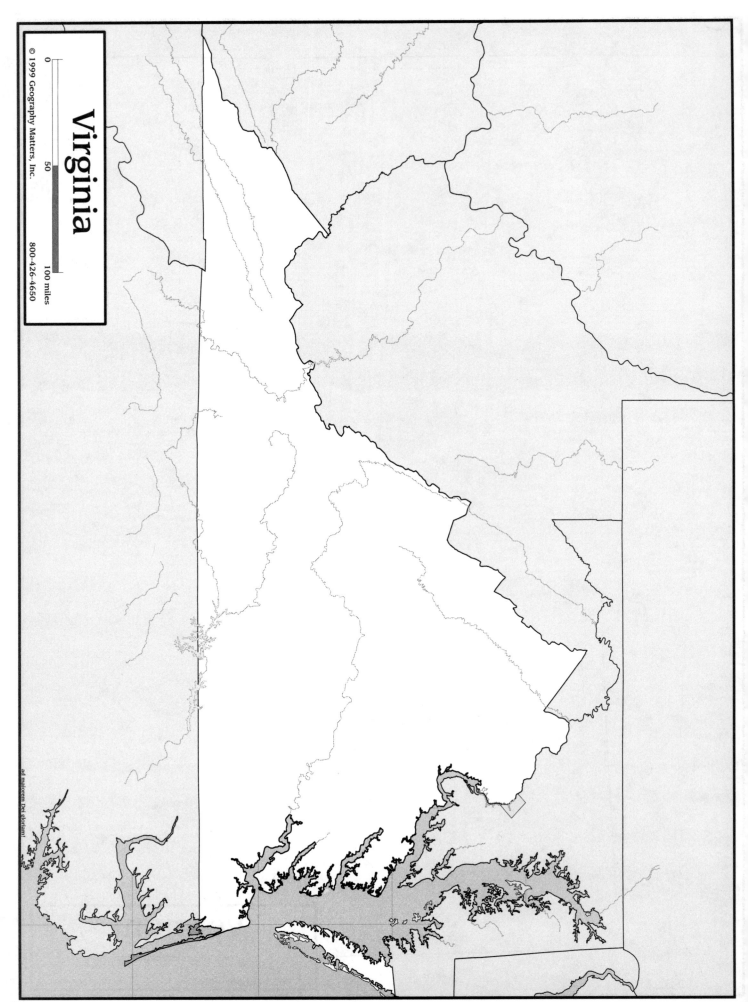

© 1999 Geography Matters, Inc.

800-426-4650

Virginia

0

50

100 miles

ad maiorem Dei gloriam!

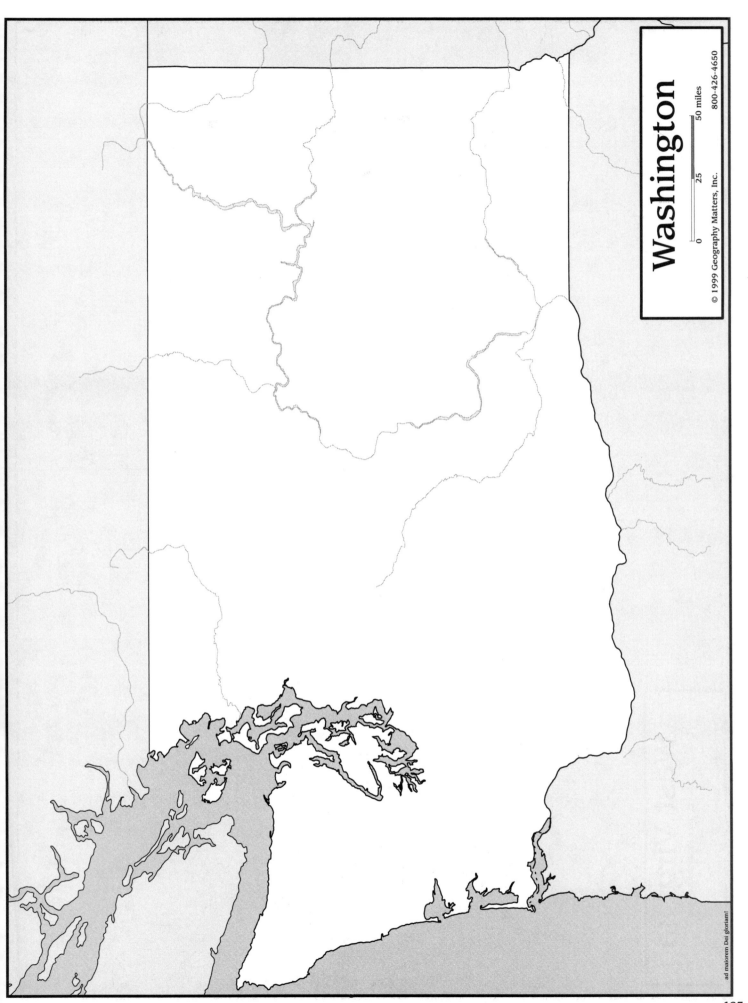

Washington

© 1999 Geography Matters, Inc.

0   25   50 miles

800-426-4650

ad maiorem Dei gloriam!

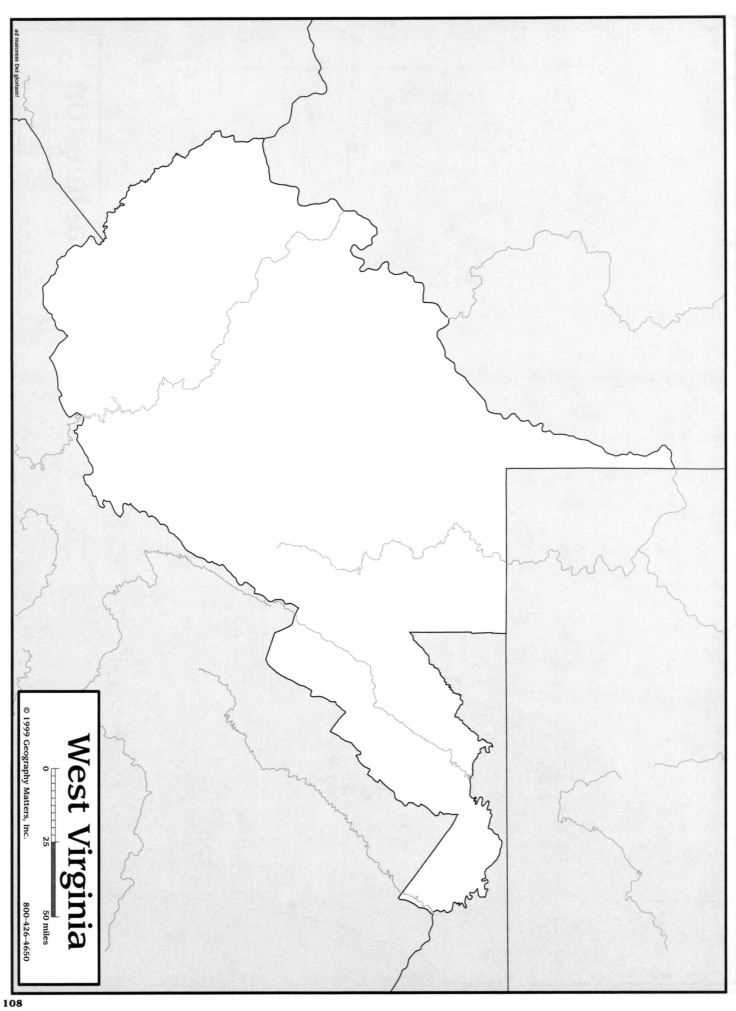

West Virginia

© 1999 Geography Matters, Inc.   800-426-4650

0   25   50 miles

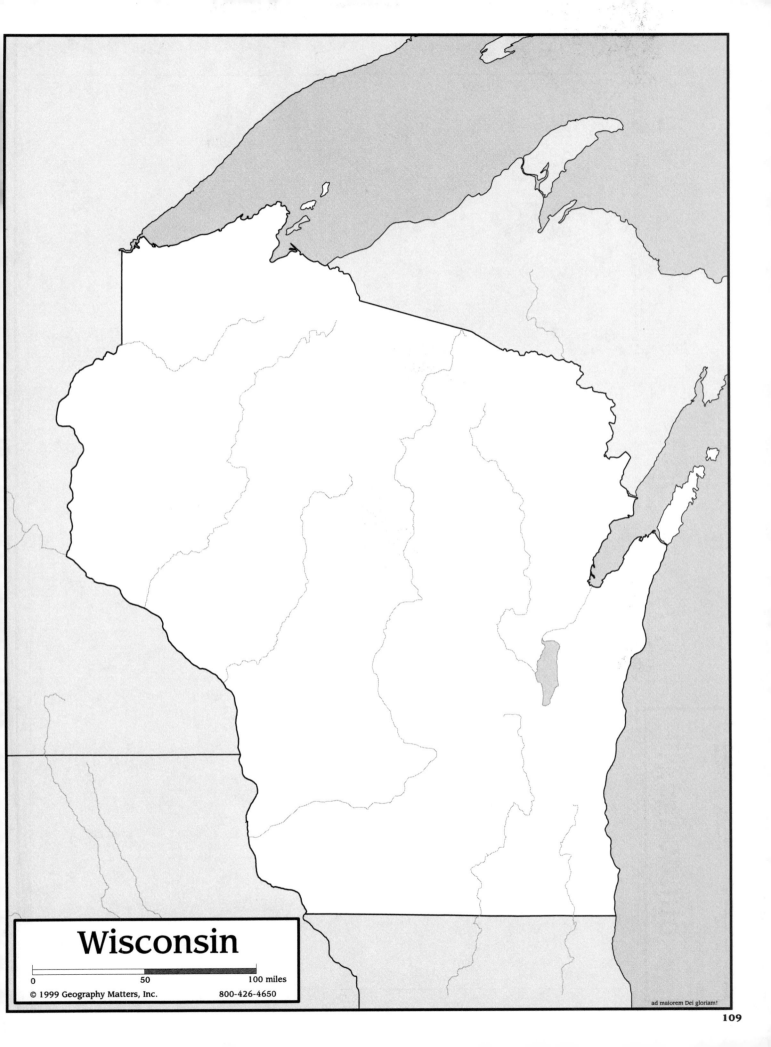

Wisconsin

0   50   100 miles

ad maiorem Dei gloriam!

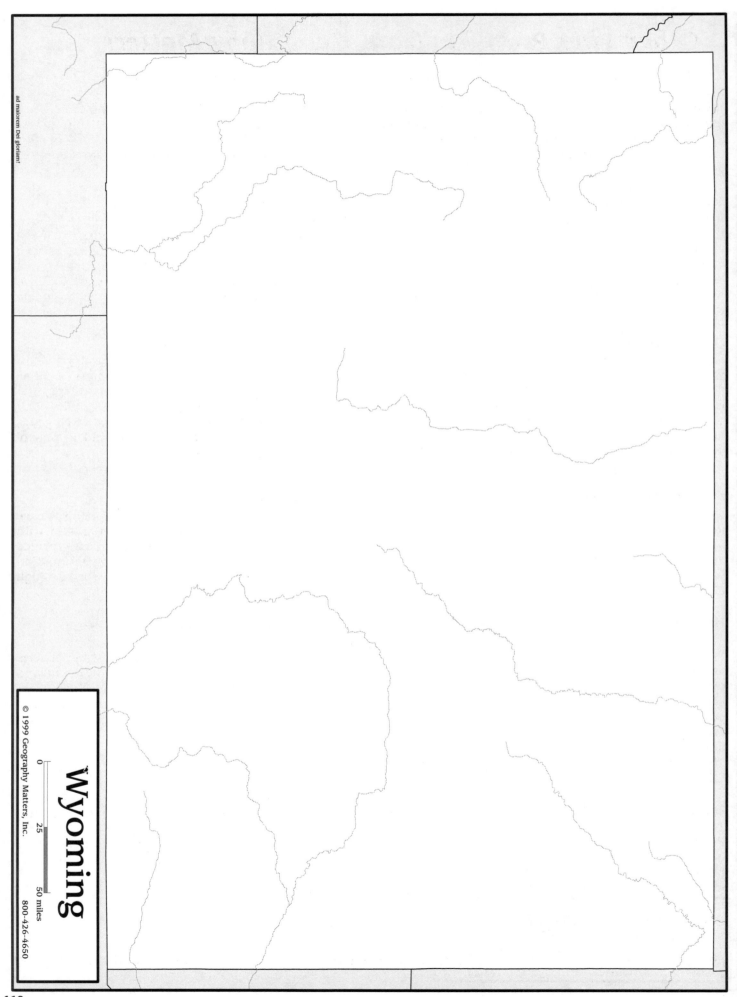

ad maiorem Dei gloriam!

Wyoming

© 1999 Geography Matters, Inc.

0   25   50 miles

800-426-4650

Other Fine Products from Geography Matters, Inc.

The Ultimate Geography and Timeline Guide
353 pages - $34.95
Need more detailed instructions on using outline maps, teaching geography and incorporating geography while studying other subjects? This is your answer! Packed with lesson plans, reproducibles, and activites geared to grades K-12.

Mark-It Desk Map Set
$16.95 paper - $34.95 laminated
If you love using outline maps but wish they were larger, these are it at 17" x 22". Recommended for use in high school curriculum or for any detailed drawing and labeling project. Seven maps include: USA, North America, South America, Africa, Europe, Israel, Ancient Civilizations.

Deluxe Mark-It Map Set
$26.95 paper - $59.95 laminated
We've covered the world in large-scale maps in this deluxe set. All seven continents are represented by: all maps in the Desk Map Set described above, PLUS a 23" x 34" double-sided map of USA and World, a 23" x 34" double-sided map of Asia and Australia (with Pacific Ocean islands) and inset of Antarctica. BONUS 23" x 34" *Mark-It Timeline of History* is also included.

Mark-It Timeline of History
23" x 34" - $9.95 laminated
Record historical data as you learn for great hands-on learning with this activity timeline poster. Dated from 4000 BC to 2050 AD on the front. The back is ready to write in your own dates for in-depth studies. Lamin-ated for durability and write-on wipe-off qualities.

Historical Timeline Figures
100 pages - $25.00
Specially designed figures feature coding to help students remember historical events. Over 350 figures include people, empires, inventions, art, music, religion, U.S. history, world events, and more. Figures are printed on perforated card stock for durability and easy removal. Generic figures provide opportunities for students to create their own. Designed to fit our **Mark-It Timeline of History**, but will work nicely on about any timeline on the market. Bonus: two games!

Hands-On Geography
100 pages - $15.00
Recommended by Cathy Duffy. This book will help you break down the geographical study of the world into bite-sized pieces. The first half of the book gives you many ideas you can use year after year: book and game making, missions and Bible study, My Country Notebook, genealogy and more. The second half is reproducible activities. Grades K-6.

Uncle Josh's Outline Map Book
112 pages - $19.95
Don't share copyrighted maps with your friends. They really should have their own book. Over 100 quality outline maps of U.S. and world. Includes one of each of the U.S. states, all continents, and major countries and regions of the world. Reproducible.

Classroom Atlas
112 pages - $9.95
Fully updated Rand McNally atlas includes Robinson projection physical and political world maps as well as thematic maps and a beautiful geography terms graphic. Excellent clear and concise artwork for ease of use. Recommended for elementary and middle school students.

Answer Atlas
176 pages - $12.95
Published by Rand McNally this all purpose atlas includes fully updated Goode's World Atlas Maps, thematic maps, and a world information section with answers to over 200 of the world's most-asked geography questions. Recommended for middle school and high school students.

Premier World Atlas
224 pages - $15.95
The most superb set of world and U.S. map art we have seen in this price range. Digital cartography with detailed country, U.S. state and Canadian province maps. The complete index makes finding information for outline activities a breeze. Recommended for high school or home library.

Gifted Children at Home
160 pages - $24.95
Your guide to searching out the best possible options for educating your gifted student! Information and hard-earned wisdom from three women who've "been there, done that." This book will encourage you and give you a firm foundation for making important educational decisions.

The Scientist's Apprentice
200 pages - $26.95
Science comes alive with this non-consumable book designed for a year's exploration of four topics: astronomy, anatomy, earth science and oceanography. Allows for teaching a variety of ages together within a flexible framework. An exciting one-year curriculum.

Contact us for our complete catalog.
Wholesale accounts welcome.

(800) 426-4650   ***www.geomatters.com***   *email: geomatters@earthlink.net*

Geography Matters, Inc.

Item	Title	Price	Qty	Total
GC100	The Ultimate Geography and Timeline Guide	$34.95		
GM903	Mark-It Desk Map Set, laminated	$34.95		
GM902	Mark-It Desk Map Set, paper	$16.95		
GM925	Deluxe Mark-It Map Set, laminated	$59.95		
GM920	Deluxe Mark-It Map Set, paper	$26.95		
GM950	Mark-It Timeline of History	$ 9.95		
LLP100	Historical Timeline Figures	$25.00		
RMANS	Answer Atlas	$12.95		
RMATL	Classroom Atlas	$ 9.95		
RMPRE	Premier World Atlas	$15.95		
GMI100	Uncle Josh's Outline Map Book	$19.95		
BI-100	Hands-On Geography	$15.00		
GG100	Gifted Children at Home	$24.95		
BI-200	The Scientist's Apprentice	$26.95		

MAIL ORDER WITH PAYMENT TO:	Shipping	$5.00
Geography Matters, Inc. P.O. Box 92 Nancy, KY 42544	Tax: KY residents add 6%	
	Total	

Ship To:

_____
Name

_____
Address

_____
City/State/Zip

_____
Phone

(800) 426-2650   www.geomatters.com

email: geomatters@earthlink.net

Payment type:
Check one   Check ____

Master Card ____   Visa ____

_____

Card #

____ / _____
Exp. Date

_____
Signature